At the Beginning

At the Beginning

Teaching Piano
to the Very Young Child

RHODA RABIN

Illustrations by Karen Foget

SCHIRMER BOOKS
An Imprint of Simon & Schuster Macmillan
NEW YORK

PRENTICE HALL INTERNATIONAL
LONDON MEXICO CITY NEW DELHI SINGAPORE SYDNEY TORONTO

Schirmer Books
An Imprint of Simon & Schuster Macmillan
866 Third Avenue
New York, NY 10022

Library of Congress Catalog Card Number: 95–34460

Printed in the United States of America

Printing number
1   2   3   4   5   6   7   8   9   10

Library of Congress Cataloging-in-Publication Data

Rabin, Rhoda.
   At the beginning : teaching piano to the very young child   /   Rhoda
Rabin.
     p.   cm.
   Includes bibliographical references and index.
   ISBN 0-02-872066-0
   1. Piano—Instruction and study—Juvenile.   I. Title.
MT745.R3   1996
786.2'07—dc20   95-34460
                                                  CIP
                                                  MN

This paper meets the requirements of ANSI-NISO Z39.48-1992 (Permanence of Paper).

To Ralph, Carol, David, Martha, Frank,
Camilla, Daniella, and Marvin

Contents

Preface

You are considering teaching piano to the very young child. Or perhaps you've already begun. Some familiar emotions attend the prospect of this enterprise. Excitement? Certainly. Exhilaration? Without a doubt.

Anxiety, too? Of course. Everyone feels it to a certain degree. Anyone who takes a profession seriously—and piano teachers certainly fit into this category—has high standards and a strong sense of responsibility. So when we consider children involved in the formal study of music, at younger ages than tradition has led us to believe is possible, it's natural to pause and think twice. After all, the role we will play in shaping young minds is a matter of enormous significance.

Everything we know, everything we have experienced, from our musicianship to our ability to empathize, is called upon when we teach the playing of the piano to young children. The temptation to question our strengths is always present. It has been present for me since the moment I began this challenging work.

Picture a freshly credentialed young teacher seated next to a four-year-old at the white-and-black expanse of a piano keyboard. During one summer at the Juilliard School of Music, Kathryne Owens, a teacher of great vision and spirit, had inspired in me the belief that this experiment could lead to wonderful results. But I still wondered: Am I equal to this? Is my young student? Can I be effective? Will the child behave? Will I?

The journey of discovery shared

Though Owens's words of wisdom were much in my thoughts, it was abundantly clear that no training, no theory, however splendid, could chart this course for me. My students and I would set out together.

This realization sometimes feels as though it happened yesterday. Teaching—perhaps music teaching in particular—is never "mastered." It is ever new, ever a process of invention and awakening, as much for ourselves as for the young people we teach. Rather than any particular method or theory, the core of that process is the relationship of the teacher and the young child.

The young student who sits so trustingly in the studio, fidgeting a little, expecting our best and deserving it, still is our surest navigator. That child's fresh exuberance reminds us over and over that building the habit of art into a life is not an ordained progress through strictly prescribed rules and methods. It is a journey of discovery.

That journey is the focus of this book.

No "method" is necessary

Don't look here for never-fail methods and rigid instructions. My hope is that you will find, instead, through suggestions, guiding rules, and affirmations, the encouragement to trust, adapt, and grow in your own skill and wisdom. I hope you will find ratification of the truths you already know, that each child is unique, carrying within himself or herself a bud of genius like no other.

The habit of art can be learned as early and well as other habits of successful living. Consider these common miracles. Any normal baby can learn to speak whatever language his parents speak, in all its detail and nuance, with a surety and swiftness that never cease to astound us. Young children can learn to share, to engineer a tower of blocks, to name the objects in their world, to persuade, to define—all tasks of infinite complexity.

In the same way they can learn to perform music. There is no secret to it, no special trick. It is in the nature of things.

How to read this book

This book can be divided informally into four sections. The first section (chapters 1–5) is devoted to background and foundation. In these chapters, I come as close as I ever do to "theory." The second section (chapters 6–10) is comprised mainly of teaching techniques and exercises. In the third section (chapters 11 and 12), I have attempted to bring together many ideas, first by describing example lessons and, second, by looking more closely at some of the more mundane, but important, considerations in the practice of piano teaching. These will, I hope, serve as a model, a guide, a framework to add to your own strategies. Finally, the appendixes (appendixes 1–3) consist of musical games and exercises. With the exception of "Hello, Ev'rybody," by Charity Bailey, these have their roots in the work of Kathryne Owens, but have been changed and adapted by me over years of teaching. They are specially designed for young children, and have been carefully presented in an order that takes into account both physical development and the sequential acquisition of essential skills.

So let us walk together on this personal journey of discovery in teaching. The children are the explorers on this journey; we are the guides. We can share with them our tools and our maps, our experiences and skills. But we don't need to predict (and who would want to?) precisely how they will use them.

It will be an enriching journey, for us as well as for our students. Young children have such an enduring ability to captivate and challenge their teachers. That is what makes our mission so important.

Acknowledgments

Special and enduring gratitude goes to Kathryne Owens, a pioneer who found new and wonderful ways to teach piano to the young child. Her classes at the Juilliard School served as an inspiration to teachers and students who had the good fortune to study with her.

I wish also to express my deep appreciation to the following people:

To Thelma Mottley, the executor of Kathryne Owens's estate, for sharing generously the wealth of materials used in this book so children for generations to come can learn from its riches.

To Donald J. Jonovic, who so patiently and determinedly believed that it was necessary for this idea to be experienced by many, and who is responsible for getting this book started and seeing it happen.

To Pamela Jonovic, for her faith in possibilities.

To Jonathan Wiener, for his belief in the importance of this book, I will always be grateful.

To my dear friend, colleague, and mentor, Alicia Downer, whose joy in teaching music through the piano has been an inspiration.

To Polly Colby, Marcia Dunscomb, Karen Foget, Amanda Vick Lethco, Annabelle Leviton, Jacquelyn Mitchard, A. Ramon Rivera, Ellyn Satter, Jean Stackhouse, Andrée Valley, Nancy Wolf, and Richard Wolf for staunch support, shared insights, and continuous encouragement.

To the memory of my parents, Irving and Sylvia Shapiro, who let music come first.

To my husband, Marvin Rabin, for his artistry, his sense of wonder, his constant challenges and powerful spirit.

To my students and their parents, who have filled my life with the music of their days.

At the Beginning

CHAPTER 1

Beginning at the Beginning

The foundations of any subject may be taught to anybody at any age in some form.
  —Jerome Bruner

What parent, given the choice, would deny very young children the experience of watering a flower and watching it grow, or hearing a wonderful story told? Why deny a child the opportunity to express music?

The child's boundless impulse to know and experience is what makes early childhood an opportune time to begin teaching music through the piano. The earlier we provide the experiences, the greater the potential for building expressions of beauty into the very fabric of as many young lives as possible.

Early piano lessons teach more than music. They go beyond keyboard technique. The benefits range far wider, into the development of the beginnings of artistry, the ability to appreciate more formally the depth and wonder of the world. That is why, in these early years, terms such as "aptitude" and "talent" are largely irrelevant. We are talking about the development of whole human beings, not specialists dedicated to one instrument or form. The potential for developing habits of ear, mind, and heart exists in every normal child.

Young children have cognitive abilities we are only beginning to understand. As teachers, we are the lens, the focus for their intellectual energy, channeling it in positive directions. We do not force children through any door; we open the door and invite them inside, with a gentleness and excitement appropriate to their ages.

What age to begin?

How young is the "young" child? For the purposes of this discussion, the young child is between three and seven years of age. I have taught students as young as two-and-a-half, however, and some have continued to study with me until they "graduated" to other teachers at the age of nine.

We know that three- or four-year-old children are reaching outward into the environment, becoming able to see themselves not just as individuals but as individuals busy *doing something*. It is important that minimum finger and motor skills exist; a child of three, at a normal level of development, has those skills.

Jerome S. Bruner, in *The Process of Education*, expressed his confidence in the ability of the young child to learn:

> Experience over the past decade points to the fact that our schools may be wasting precious years by postponing the teaching of many important subjects on the grounds that they are too difficult.
>
> . . . My position is based on the proposition that the foundations of any subject may be taught to anybody at any age in some form. Though this proposition may seem startling at first, its intent is to underscore an essential point, often overlooked in the planning of a curriculum.
>
> It is that the basic ideas that are at the heart of all science and mathematics, and the basic themes that give form to life and literature are as simple as they are powerful. To be in command of these basic ideas, to use them effectively, requires a continual deepening of one's understanding of them that comes from learning to use them in progressively more complex forms.

Think, in this same context, of the early teaching of piano as the foundation of a great castle. Think of "keyboard-ese" as a musical alphabet. The foundation we are building is not of mortar or stone, but of aesthetics. We are imbuing children with the habit of art through music.

Look at the ways children tell us they are ready to wel-

come music into their lives. They bob in their seats to songs they hear, they hum and sing long before they speak. They delight in the differences and qualities of sound as they ring a bell or drum on a cooking pot. Their natural desire to perform is the dominant theme of many families' home videos. Young children like to be shown how to use materials, and they communicate naturally through movement and play. Of additional benefit to the teaching process is the fact that many young children have not yet learned to be self-conscious or shy, so they often can perform together with a sense of sharing, without competition.

For children, the piano is one more tool for discovery. Young children respond immediately to this special music machine that brings forth such beguiling new sounds.

Early piano lessons build on natural abilities already present in each child. When children learn that it's possible to express awe, excitement, and emotion with another medium besides the voice, beyond crayons and finger paints, it is often a joyful revelation.

Why the piano?

The benefits of that revelation are priceless, and they can last a lifetime. Even those children who do not continue with the formal study of piano beyond the early years find that the understanding they have gained is never erased. I have followed many of the students who began with me when they were very young, and almost every one continued with music in some form later in life—on the piano or another instrument or voice.

Whether they listen or whether they play, there will always be music in their lives.

The assumption here is that we've chosen to introduce children to music through the medium of the piano, this huge cabinet with its 88 keys. Wouldn't a small violin be a more manageable first choice for such a young child?

Yet, the choice of the piano is eminently sensible. Of primary importance is the fact that the piano gives music so readily. It is no accident that the classic toy instrument is a piano, and that the cartoonist Charles Schulz's young character Schroeder dreams of Beethoven while he taps away at three toy keys.

With the piano, a child of three can go home playing a song after the first lesson. As Pablo Casals wrote,

> I am glad I learned the piano at the very beginning. For me it is the best of all instruments. Yes, despite my love of the cello. On a piano you can play anything that has been written. The instrument encompasses everything.
>
> It encompasses, for example, the full spectrum of sound and an infinite flexibility in harmony, put together in a form that allows a child to really see and understand the logical relationships among sounds.

Also consider that:

• A piano is easily negotiated. A child can move easily

around a keyboard, and you, at the child's side, have a clear field for demonstration.

- The piano is always in the same place. You can't lose it on the bus or forget about it by putting it away in the closet.
- Piano keys are fixed pitches, and are easily located and repeated. A child can find and repeat a sound without the frustration of a tonal search.

The child is our model

There are social and historical reasons for focusing on the piano as the instrument of choice for the young child. As David Barnett, a professor of piano at the New England Conservatory of Music, Wellesley College, and Harvard and Columbia Universities, wrote in *The Performance of Music:*

> It is the predominant instrument among amateurs. It draws the most students in colleges, conservatories and music schools. It is freqently studied as a second instrument by players of other instruments. In contrast to string instruments, it has been retained for a variety of purposes by composers and players of popular music . . .

New piano teachers, just beginning to work with young children, are often as awed by the responsibility as they are excited by the challenge. Men and women who choose such a profession tend to be highly motivated and serious about their standards.

The natural tendency, under these conditions, is to depend heavily on books and papers, rules and maxims, prepackaged techniques and exercises. The new teacher often holds tightly to these tools, seeing them as insurance that young students will get the quality teaching they deserve.

Inexperience can lead to dependence on structured frameworks and methods that do help ensure that a teacher becomes—and stays—an effective teacher. Knowledge *is* important, of course. Sensitivity, skill, and the ability to empathize and communicate are important, too. But a constrictive, inflexible method tends to plane away a child's uniqueness, leaving behind shavings that represent some of the best in each emerging mind.

The best model for all of us is, in fact, the young person

who sits next to us in the studio. It is this child who provides the focus for all of our work. No method is advocated here, nor will the reader find prescriptions, rules, or lists of restrictions. No universal rules exist for teaching the young child. In the place of rules is one simple truth: *Just as there is no single definition of intelligence, there is no typical or average child.*

Children are not merely raw material. They are active partners in a process of exploration and discovery, and they have an almost infinite capacity to surprise even the most experienced teacher. This is the source of our challenge as teachers. It is also what brings us the greatest joy.

The abilities are readily accessible

There is much to learn. As with anyone on a voyage of discovery, teachers of young children can learn much from older explorers of the territory. More important, however, we have our own knowledge, skill, and instinct to help us find our way, which we continuously must expand and refine. We must learn and discover for ourselves.

Fortunately, the safest course for teachers and parents is to trust instinct. Doubt and uncertainty spring from a single failure: the failure to believe in the rightness of feelings and instincts we have about the children with whom we work. The fact is, these feelings are deeply rooted and are reliable guides. *A basic and continuing message to both parents and teachers is to trust the power of your own wisdom.*

Vast, as yet untapped potentials exist within the fresh, active, absorbent mind of every young child, and there is no doubt that the young child can learn and grow as a piano student.

As teachers, we have the privilege of exploring those potentials with each child we meet. "Pre-piano" or music readiness classes are unnecessary. The gifts of the piano are readily accessible and young children are ready to explore them. They can go directly to the instrument and find all the early music training they need incorporated, organically and immediately, in the actual experience of playing the piano.

CHAPTER 2

Art and the Art Habit

The object of art is to give life a shape.
—Jean Anouilh

What is the "art habit"? It is the love for and practice of art, the incorporating of formal expressions of beauty into the life of an individual, in our case, the young child. Our objective with early piano lessons is to develop the art habit in children, and to make the piano as natural a part of life as the telephone or the bicycle.

The cornerstone of teaching music to the young child is the absolute belief that young children can be accomplished artists: accomplished not in terms of the size or complexity of their repertoire, but in terms of their ability to produce beautiful sounds and respond to beauty, in learned as well as instinctive ways. Is it naïve or overly romantic, this idea of the child as artist? Experience shows that it is not. Whether or not a child is precocious in other areas of his or her life, he or she can make music and experience the extraordinary dimension this power lends to a young life.

Young students are as deserving of the finest artistic instruction as conservatory students are. From the first moment the child touches the keys, we are teaching art—not "art readiness."

We have the opportunity to begin fostering the love of music and performance just at the time that youngsters are beginning to experience themselves as individuals, individuals who want the thrill of being able to do something special

and important. And yet, they have very little control over their environment. This works to our advantage. As teachers, we are able to present this wonderful gift of the piano before the other attractive elements of early life (school activities, clubs and scouting, sports, even video games!) take too strong a hold. The art habit, once rooted in a child's spirit, is not easily dislodged. Waiting to begin until a child's life is diversified (and this happens soon enough) is an option, but one that may yield diminished artistic returns.

The instructional guides and techniques we use to introduce and nurture the art habit in the young child do not trammel creativity; they release it. As poets and philosophers have said for centuries, real freedom of action or expression is possible only in the context of rules. This powerful paradox has everything to do with the reason that early piano teaching proves so successful.

Though they are very young when they come to us, children are already comfortable with the concept of rules. Games for them have rules. If you doubt this, try varying the rules the next time you play with a young child! Even the youngest child who is learning to speak sees how the rules of grammar enhance the power of verbal communication. We empower our students to express themselves musically by sharing the routines and conventions of music.

Music study is only one area of life in which the acquisition of routines helps realize important objectives. We should think of the art habit as a goal that can be attained not just in a rarefied atmosphere but in the context of the many habits and routines we expect the young child to learn as part of the growth process. We teach a young child to use a toothbrush, a simple task with the important goal of life-long health. We teach a child to share, with the goal of life-long civility in dealing with other people. We teach a child to play piano with the objective of instilling the lifelong appreciation of beauty through musical expression. This is an objective no more exalted, but just as important to full and fruitful life as any of the other healthful habits.

When does the art habit begin?

The art habit begins the day we first open our eyes (some would say even before), and as teachers we are continuing that process with the student. What are some of the elements of the art habit? Preparation, respect, ritual, scheduling, and precision all combine to give beauty a form and a voice in our lives.

Don't let the term "precision" stop you. I am not referring to *perfection*, an inappropriate goal for a young child. But teaching *precision*—the knowledge that, in music, things can be accomplished every time in an exact and predictable way—is important. Our students will not achieve perfection every time, and, in fact, mistakes are important turns in the road, real occasions for learning.

Teaching children precision in music study is the first step to mastery, which we think of as a feeling of ease. We can help guide our students to mastery, to ease with their bodies and their instruments in performance by teaching the habit of precision.

And just as a kindergarten or early elementary-school teacher, introducing children to the experience of writing, praises the wonderful ideas and deemphasizes the misspellings, we, too, praise process over product. Success builds on success. In addition, allowing our students to know that even we, powerful adults, are liable to make mistakes helps to build their self-esteem.

The refinement of the product comes with time and experience, but we see clearly, almost immediately, the extreme importance that the growth of a new skill has in the child. We're all thrilled to hear that familiar cry, "Look! I can do it myself!" That is the beginning of mastery. Children want mastery and they are able to acquire it.

The following chapters will expand the discussion of the techniques and instructional guides used to foster the art habit in the young child. Let us turn now to the most critical elements of the process, the people who provide the framework in which the art habit takes root and begins to flourish.

CHAPTER 3

The Child

The best way to make children good is to make them happy.
—*Oscar Wilde*

The door opens, and in walks an independent universe—a young child, different from any other, your student.

Young children learn instinctively, from the middle out, as it were. Intellectually, they grasp most easily the things they feel most fully. Show them, allow them to feel, and you allow them to learn. The way a young child learns makes the relationship between the child and the teacher the most critical element of early music lessons. Our task as teachers is to understand and absorb the geography of our students, just as we teach them to absorb the geography of the keyboard. We can teach young children to be piano-friendly because we are child-friendly. We become child-friendly in part simply because we like and respect young children, but also because we've taken the time, as teachers, to remember how young children differ, as students, from adults and older children.

In the studio, the child is the focus of all the proceedings. The child's world—the child's interests, delights and habits—is the primary concern. Children are bright, intuitive human beings. They aren't gullible; we have to earn their trust by showing them elaborate courtesy and genuine willingness to help and to care. Young children will instantly identify a phony. They sense intuitively the important distinction between being praised and being patronized, between genuine interest in their lives and the mere pretense of interest.

If we approach them on their level, not as a playmate but as a true friend with gifts of learning to share, they will return our trust in them and return our respect. And we will have placed one more brick in the strong foundation of helping a child build a healthy, confident interaction with the world.

Let's consider some of the characteristics of small children:

- Mental and physical growth is rapid.
- Physical coordination is increasing.
- Reality is distinguished from the imaginary.
- Concentration span is limited.
- Impulses are manageable.
- Information is used to define an individual persona.
- Learning depends to a great extent on imitation.
- Physical activity is important and essential to learning.
- Desire for praise is powerful.
- Memory is quick . . . and shallow.
- Interaction is frank and loquacious.
- Curiosity runs high.
- Reality is seen in relation to self.
- Vocabulary is wide and growing.
- Group instincts, sociability and gregariousness are present and can be encouraged.
- Taking turns is usually an accepted part of life.
- Demonstration work is very important.
- The desire to please is strong.
- Learning takes place quickly . . . and slowly.
- "Age exclusivity" is not yet an important factor.
- Skills are developing at an earlier age.

Mental and physical growth is rapid

Young children are growing mentally and physically faster than they will at any other time in their lives. They're changing in their relationship to the world, too. Children are often ready for lessons when they demonstrate that they can spend time, working alone with an adult other than a parent, in a room separate from the parent, although it's a great idea

for parents always to be nearby. That threshold most often occurs between two-and-a-half and three years of age. Many children at this age are capable of learning, at different rates, to make music from symbols (i.e, to "read music"), although care must be taken to present the symbols to them in an appropriate manner.

A three-year-old in May is a very different character from that same three-year-old in September, just five months later. At four, along will come a different sort of person, another at five. Children ordinarily grow about three inches a year during early childhood. We can create a visible symbol of progress and the longevity of our learning relationship for children by making seasonal height marks, labeled for each child, on a door frame or other suitable charting place. "See how far we've come together," these marks seem to say.

The way children use these growing bodies is changing rapidly, as well. Because we know, for example, that one child may have already picked up the behavior of raising a hand before answering a question while another has not, we can be sensitive to those differences, instead of interpreting them as distractions or lack of interest in the lesson.

We can use our understanding of these different ranges of mental, social, and physical growth as opportunities to teach, recognizing the important truth that in young students' worlds, small incidents take on more profound significance than those same incidents will even a year or two from now.

Physical coordination is increasing

Refinements in young children's physical skills happen almost daily. Gross motor skills, such as throwing a ball and dancing, change dramatically during these years, improving week to week. Small motor skills, including tying a shoelace and holding a pencil (and playing the piano!), also develop rapidly over a single season.

We take advantage of the child's growing body control—especially, but not specifically, the control of the hand and arm—with many exercises based on knowledge of kinesthetics. The objective is to help each child develop ease with his body.

That ease, as we know, is a primary component of becoming piano-friendly. So is the eye-hand relationship, a developmental skill children learn from birth and refine in early childhood.

Developmental realities naturally guide the pacing of lessons. For example, prior to about age three, most children use their fingers as a fist. Between ages three and four, it becomes possible to begin individualizing the fingers.

Children can understand pitch differences even if they cannot reproduce them vocally. Frequently, the young child's physical ability to produce specific sounds can't keep up with his ability to hear and discern the differences among sounds. But it often is the vocal apparatus, not the musical sensibility, that is undeveloped before about the age of three.

Thanks to this recognition of the wide variations in normal development, we can reassure students and parents and nip such damaging myths as the "tone deaf" child before they ever get started.

Reality is distinguishable from the imaginary

Children, of course, are imagination factories, and the younger they are, the more powerful and pervasive is the role of imagination in their lives. But do children have difficulty separating reality from fantasy in a learning environment? No, in general, they do not.

Of course, we can make the distinction easier. The word "silly" can be a wonderful teaching friend. It can be used to distinguish between things done for fun ("being silly") and things that are real ("non-silly"). For example, in the studio, an exercise in which children imagine that they are seesaws is a "silly" visualization with an important rhythmic and developmental purpose underlying it. But learning about the black keys on the piano (three black friends and two black friends side by side) is a "non-silly" concept.

Concentration span is limited

Just as a child learns to absorb literature through the repetition of a favorite story, a young child studying music can be guided by familiar routine and repetition. We can take advantage of the limits of children's attention by frequently changing the focus, subject, and physical position within the context of the lesson's routine.

Little boys generally require more changes in position and movement than little girls do, and it may be easier, at first, to keep girls focused on the piano. But though boys' attention span may be different at first, the differences lessen with time, and we can provide more activities that demand more concentration.

When children know what to expect, they can focus more clearly and attend to each activity more easily. Just as they understand and relish the patterns of a bedtime story, they can easily come to understand the design of the lesson set up for their needs and know that after listening comes technique, and after technique, finger games, and then on to the piano. The lesson has its rhythm, and the child comes to "play in tune" with that rhythm.

Impulses are manageable

With the right amount of leadership and direction from the teacher, who always emphasizes the positive and guides the way from one activity to the next, children can learn to turn their natural exuberance toward productive results. Our challenge is to be sensitive to the child's emotions, and understand that most emotional impulses have underlying causes.

Is someone feeling low on a particularly gloomy day? Perhaps, since we often best express our emotions through song, it's good to begin that day's lesson by singing—going with the mood instead of against it. Is your student excited, filled with wiggles on a particular day? Let the child lead, and fill that day's lesson with more standing and movement than usual.

We often find that "listening" to children's body language leads to a more satisfying and meaningful lesson than any attempt to control those impulses.

Information is used to define an individual persona

A young child gradually becomes conscious of being an individual separate from parents, distinct from the whole environment. This expanded consciousness of self can lead to "self-consciousness," which can affect the teaching process positively. As they grow, young children are increasingly able to see music as a medium for expressing their own ideas.

By reaching them early and making the experience of performing together an occasion for sharing instead of competing, we can hedge against the potential for developing shyness, and help children see musical performance as an activity just as natural as participating in sports or reading aloud.

Learning depends to a great extent on imitation _____

From observing what we all know about the young child's remarkable ability to learn language through a natural ability to imitate sounds and expressions, we see a tremendous opportunity to build musical response by imitation through the medium of the piano.

As teachers, we observe how our students imitate their parents, their older siblings, and the other important people in their lives. Since we are now one of those important people—someone the child may see more frequently during a week's time than anyone except family members or teachers at nursery school or elementary school—we can take advantage of this wish to imitate us as well.

Beware! Children are powerful, intuitive mimes, and you may well see yourself reflected in the personality of your young student at the piano. The importance of your behavioral example, as an artist and as a teacher, cannot be underestimated.

Physical activity is important and essential to learning _____

Mastery play, sensory play, and rough-and-tumble play are the learning tools of early childhood. Expending energy through play helps children develop their bodies and their minds, and it is a process that you can encourage steadily in the studio. Let them play during music lessons, because play directed toward the love and performance of music is a great force for learning.

Desire for praise is powerful _____

Life will do its best to teach children about disappointment. We are in the business of teaching them the joy of feeling success. We give every child the gift of leaving a lesson feeling that he has pleased himself, pleased us, and learned something important—no matter how the lesson has gone in strictly technical terms.

Young children value praise, and we must never assume that they already know they're doing well. It's literally possible to praise a child for almost everything that the child does in class. When they leave, they will be buoyed up by the recognition of their strengths and not anxious about their shortcomings. They will be eager to return. The lesson will be a happy place where learning is accomplished in the presence of confidence and joy.

Memory is quick . . . and shallow

Young children absorb information readily but without much analysis. Consequently, though they may remember information, it is not always readily integrated with the knowledge they already possess and use.

For the young child, the psychological system that works best is a framework that builds upward steadily, step by step, each step intimately linked to the one before in an observable pattern. Each exercise changes subtly, incorporating the knowledge that came before. In this way, changes or successive tasks "fit" the scheme. They're more readily stored and used.

As the years pass, the ability to retain learned material grows markedly. Between the ages of four-and-a-half and five it soars, and a repertoire at this stage can consist of 40 pieces or more.

Interaction is frank and loquacious

Young children tell it as they see it. They don't possess the adult equipment that makes it possible to obfuscate for the sake of politeness. They may confide in you that the moon whirled past their window at high speed the night before and, from their point of view, that's an accurate description. They may volunteer, quite seriously, the most astonishing information, such as the child who, when I used my fingers as the musical staff and asked what was between them, responded cheerfully, "Dirt!"

Young children exercising their powerful new faculty are extremely talkative. Sometimes, the things they say can sound harsh in adult terms, but they almost never intend those things to be hurtful. Most often, their pointed "suggestions" can be useful.

Curiosity runs high

We all know that young children get into things. As an example, while plants should make the waiting area a pleasant, cheerful place, expect a curious child to go digging at some point. Such situations are occasions for guidance. We can take advantage of young children's natural affinity for "anthropomorphism" (assigning human characteristics to everything around them) by suggesting that we help the plants stay healthy by keeping their "toes" in the earth.

Curiosity may be directed at you. "Why do you wear glasses?" a child may ask, or "Is your sweater itchy?" The best policy is to treat curiosity naturally and simply, supplying appropriate information and setting fair limits.

Reality is seen in relation to self

A child I knew once asked a parent, "Why do they put a pit in every cherry? We just have to throw it away." Another complained, "Why does it still have to be light outside? Doesn't the sun know it's bedtime?" Statements like these are common from children ages two-and-a-half to six. They see the world differently than adults do, and so, differently than their teacher. Most of us remember feeling just this way, and we recognize how the child's strength and vulnerability run parallel as he or she grows and how important our interactions with the child are in fostering a sense of being special in the world. Discussing these matters together draws us closer to our students. They are delighted to meet an adult willing to listen to their theories.

Vocabulary is wide and growing

Many young children today have been exposed to the influence of mass media from the cradle. They often have vocabularies that include thousands of words, including a fair number of polysyllabic words. Though we don't try to speak with them as though they were miniature adults, our communication with them can be extremely rich, complex, and varied. That communication, and the visible expression of the way we relate to one another, is of inestimable value in our teaching.

A teacher's recognition of the fact that children love to make up words (one student taught me, for example, that the combination of "stockings" and "socks" is "stocks") can be a special bond between teacher and student. Use the made-up words in a song. "Jeremy's stocks are filled with blocks, so what will he wear to play to-DAY!" Fuse one form of joy, word invention, with another, making music.

Group instinct, sociability, and gregariousness are present and can be encouraged

The great majority of young students are naturally outgoing. We can encourage the tendency to share music and artistry spontaneously, through performance and group lessons that include ensemble playing. We want our students to connect with each of them before they have a chance to become shy or introverted. Relating well with one another is not just a by-product of the lesson; it is an integral part of the lesson.

Even children who have a personality that tends to be more reserved can easily make music a part of their social life. Sharing music with one another can ease their interactions with others throughout their lives.

Taking turns is usually an accepted part of life

Watch a group of young children at play and their understanding of give-and-take in social situations is readily revealed. Young children in a group easily accept the necessity for everyone to have a chance to answer or ask questions in their turn.

Demonstration is very important

Showing and telling children how and why the piano makes such beautiful sounds only increases children's respect for the instrument. Similarly, showing them the keyboard concepts of "high" and "low" and "up" and "down" by asking them to stand or sit on their chairs at the appropriate moment creates a harmony between the location of the body in space and the location of the keyboard in music.

The desire to please is strong

Questions about behavior are among the most common concerns piano teachers express when they begin working with very young children. This worry is unnecessary. Children at this age get a great deal of satisfaction from seeing your satisfaction. In the proper setting, with the right kind of encouragement and structure, young children's dominant desire to please an important, caring adult will mean that they will follow instuctions cheerfully and try hard to do well.

Learning takes place quickly . . . and slowly

One day, a student will astonish you by grasping a concept within minutes that often takes weeks to establish. The next day, the same student may seem unable to "connect" with another, simpler concept.

As teachers, we understand that children's ability to process various kinds of information is not uniform at this or perhaps any age. Maturity doesn't happen suddenly. It evolves, and we respect this process when we resist the temptation to hurry—making sure we demonstrate first and explain later.

"Age exclusivity" is not yet an important factor

A fifth-grader might scorn the third-grade neighborhood buddy he considered a fast friend last summer. Peer pressure can be a factor. Younger children, however, seem to get along well with slightly younger or older children, sharing group music activity in an atmosphere that encourages such sharing. So if you have been working successfully with six-year-olds, one rule of thumb is to dial back one year. Try a five-year-old first. Then a four-year-old. Though we would not pair a three-year-old with a six-year-old who had two years of lessons, pairing a four- and five-year-old who are both beginners usually works very well. The older child takes a natural leadership role and the younger one is encouraged by example to try new things.

Skills are developing at an earlier age

Before *Sesame Street*, we may have underestimated young children's adaptability and ability to learn. The increased interest in early childhood education has enriched the environment for today's young children and given us, as piano teachers, opportunities to explore new potentials and horizons.

We are fortunate indeed to be teaching at a time in history when the interest in fostering early experiences of learning is such an important part of our culture.

CHAPTER 4

The Family

We teachers can only help the work going on, as servants wait upon a master.
—Maria Montessori

A successful piano experience for the young child includes the child, the teacher, and the parents. Like a three-legged stool, the student and the teacher are two of the legs, but the parents balance and support the whole endeavor.

If young children sense that their parents respect and like the teacher, that we're a team, it infuses the whole atmosphere with a fine sense of cordiality.

In the best of all possible worlds, parents participate actively in their child's music study—not in the studio lesson itself, but in the support, encouragement, and monitoring that take place at home.

As teachers, we owe it to parents to let them know that they will have to work alongside the child to make this whole process successful. They will be our eyes and ears at home. We will have to rely on them to let us know all the changing influences in a child's environment that will have an impact on the study of music. Parents are partners in this enterprise, and they usually are eager to do all they can.

When we discuss what we need to provide for parents, it is important to consider:

- The introductory interview
- Informing the parents of their roles at the lesson and at home
- Establishing an atmosphere of free communication

The introductory interview

Before the first lesson ever takes place, before the child and the teacher even meet, the teacher must have a good idea of how well a child will "take" to the piano. Even though children are not auditioned, I rarely refuse or discontinue a student. It is possible to obtain much of the information needed to work with the child from early discussions with the parents. In a sense, it is the parents who are auditioned.

What do we, as teachers, hope for in "piano parents"?

We hope to find parents who care about music, whether they play or not, and who are deeply interested in the experiences they give to their children. Fortunately, the parents who bring their children to us for lessons are usually such involved, supportive parents.

At some point before the first lesson, it is necessary to meet with both parents, without the child if possible, to learn about the prospective student and the environment in which he or she lives. This also is the time for parents to ask questions about your philosophy and policies. This meeting is an occasion for making everyone feel comfortable in the context of sharing information.

There are some questions to ask, as well as points to be raised, and they are outlined in the sample interview that follows, along with the rationale behind each of them.

• HOW OLD IS THE CHILD? Find out not just the age, but the child's birth date and whether he or she has had any exposure to nursery school or kindergarten. It's not necessary for them to have had any schooling, of course, but it's useful to know in planning lessons and scheduling.

• ARE THERE BROTHERS AND SISTERS? Determine how old each sibling is, what schools the other children attend, and whether they play instruments. This is valuable information for role modeling, evaluating other influences, and even for arranging future ensemble playing.

• DO YOU OR YOUR SPOUSE PLAY ANY MUSICAL INSTRUMENTS OR DO YOU ENJOY SINGING? Again, reassure parents that it's certainly not necessary that they be accomplished musicians to help their child succeed with piano lessons; it's not necessary that they play at all. But if one parent plays a saxophone or a harmonica, or sings, you can help construct opportunities for them to play or sing along with their children. If the parents took piano lessons as children or express interest in learning the piano, make it a point to arrange a way for them to learn some rudimentary things to play along with their child. It's a delightful plus for both the student and parent. Parents' interest in exposing their child to music frequently leads them to study piano as well.

• WE MEET FOR AT LEAST TWO SESSIONS A WEEK. Parents who expect the traditional model of one piano lesson each week need to understand how difficult it can be for the young child to be exposed to something new and extraordinary, and then be expected to work alone on that task for seven long days between lessons. Explain that even three short lessons are not uncommon in the first years, and that the multiple sessions allow the young child to "practice" at the studio. Explain that all lessons are one-on-one at first, and the second lesson becomes a group lesson after the first several weeks.

• THIS IS THE WAITING ROOM WHERE YOU'LL SPEND TIME WHEN YOUR CHILD IS IN THE STUDIO. Let parents know that they'll always be nearby during the lesson, but that it is important for the lesson itself to take place in a private setting that emphasizes the intimacy between teacher and student. Point out the books, toys, and other materials available for parents, students, and younger siblings to use while they wait. Include the location of the telephone and restroom. Emphasize that the waiting room is a place to be comfortable. Explain that questions and discussions about the child's progress are best handled on the telephone instead of at lessons, because children often grow impatient with "adult" talk, and the teacher often needs to move along to the next lesson.

• TELL ME ABOUT YOUR PIANO. This is the time to ask parents where their piano is located, when it was last tuned, and whether they are satisfied with the tuner they currently use.

Parents need to embrace the importance of having the best instrument they can afford. They should understand the necessity of tuning it twice a year, and that the piano tuner can be a good source of information on products such as pedal extenders and special stools that give young children the best access to the pedals and support their feet. You can tell parents about various types of pianos. You also can recommend *A Piano Book* by Larry Fine (see Bibliography) and provide a list of reliable dealers for music products and instruments. Explain, too, the importance of location of the instrument in the piano-friendly household (see "At home," p. 30).

• I'D LIKE TO TELL YOU ABOUT LESSON SCHEDULING AND COMMITMENTS. In general, it seems that parents who are led to understand the importance of showing up regularly do just that. Children usually can't "make up" missed days of nursery or elementary school if they go on vacation with the family or have another reason to be away, and you should stress that music lessons are similar to other educational experiences (see "Schedule Lesson Times" below).

• LET'S DISCUSS TUITION. Payment is made in advance, with no refund for missed lessons (see above). But parents have the option of paying for the entire school year, by semesters, or monthly. In any group of parents, several choose each of the options. You may have other methods that work well for you.

• I WANT TO TELL YOU ABOUT SOME OF THE MOST ENJOYABLE EVENTS OF THE YEAR, THOSE TIMES WHEN STUDENTS HAVE THE CHANCE TO PLAY FOR ONE ANOTHER AND FOR THEIR FAMILIES. WE CALL THEM PIANO PARTIES. Explain why the term "recital" may not be the most appropriate for the young child, and how you consider these periodic celebrations of music occasions of joy, not exams. The children look forward to piano parties with great anticipation. Give parents some idea of when they are scheduled—for example, at Halloween, before winter holiday break, on Valentine's Day, and just before school ends in the spring.

• YOU'LL WANT TO KNOW ABOUT MATERIALS. Use this time to explain your procedures for providing printed music, assignment books, and other materials. It's best for the teacher to purchase and provide music and other materials at the lessons and bill parents later. That way students receive all their materials without delay when they need them.

Tell parents the child will need to bring little slippers, clipped together and labeled with the child's name, to wear in the studio. These protect the piano from shoe tips and also provide a ritual of entrance into a new environment, like removing shoes before entering a Japanese home. Also inform the parents about providing blank cassette tapes for recording the child's performances and playing in certain lessons throughout the school year. The child will also need a bag for carrying his or her supplies (see Materials and Equipment, chapter 7).

• NOW LET'S SCHEDULE THE LESSON TIMES. You can make suggestions about the regular times that work best for you each week, but in general it's up to you to adapt your schedule as best you can to the schedule of these busy families. Since you are working with young children, many of whom may not yet be in full-day school, you may not need to schedule as many evening and Saturday hours as teachers of piano traditionally do (see also "Lesson Scheduling" above).

Another matter about which parents express concern is summer lessons. Although some teachers make summer classes a great occasion for music fun and experimentation, many others find it works best to schedule piano class alongside the traditional school calendar with a break in the summer. You can assure parents, however, that children don't lose their piano knowledge over the summer and return refreshed and ready to work when fall arrives.

• I'M VERY INTERESTED IN KNOWING JUST WHAT YOUR HOPES ARE ABOUT YOUR CHILD IN STUDYING PIANO. This is your golden opportunity to find out just what parents expect and hope to realize from music lessons. Do they hope to raise a prodigy? Do they think their child has musical talent? Do they think music is simply an enjoyable and important part of life? Since the attitude of the parents is so critical, they reveal a great deal by their answers, and you, in turn, have the chance to explain your philosophy of teaching the young child. This also can be the opportunity to reassure parents that children who can participate in the simplest preschool setting often are ready for piano lessons, and to share with them your definition of musical mastery and musical success as they relate to the young child.

In sum, the introductory interview is the place at which all your instincts and people-sense come into play. When I tell teachers that in my years of teaching I've declined to teach only a very few children, they're often surprised and curious. In those cases, it was really the parents with whom I felt I couldn't work successfully. You should rely on your intuition; if the parents are uncooperative and you don't feel they support you fully, then you should consider not working with them. In general, "piano parents" are the best kind of parents. Bear in mind you're working directly with one young student, but in the larger sense, you are educating a whole family.

Additional information for the parents

Teaching piano to the young child is an involved, holistic process. Parents need to know what will be expected of them in this context. There are many things to absorb at the beginning.

At the lesson   Parents wonder why they need to be present for every lesson. One reason is to nurture the confidence of the child; another is to enable parents to hear what their child is learning and how, so they can offer support and encouragement on the days between lessons.

Many parents have asked me why so much talking and so little playing seems to go on during early lessons. In time, parents fully endorse the idea that everything that goes on in the lesson, no matter how seemingly unrelated, nurtures the study of music. They need to understand that the teacher is an important adult in the child's life, a confidante and friend, and the relationship becomes a vital part of the learning atmosphere. It is important, then, for you to ask how

Grandma's visit is going, what's new at school, how the tree house is progressing.

Occasionally, teaching methods themselves might result in opportunities for increasing parents' understanding. A father once questioned me about requiring his young son to stand rather than sit at the keyboard while the child played. When I explained that standing, far from being awkward or uncomfortable, actually affords a three-year-old the best position for negotiating the entire keyboard, he accepted the need for this. There are many other chances to share the reasons why the methods we use are so helpful in giving the child the best possible experience, even though those methods may seem untraditional at first.

Though a half hour is allotted for each lesson, there may be times in the early days when a child stays in the studio only eight or ten minutes. Parents who feel concerned about a lesson that seems too short need to understand how important it is to let a child leave before that child is bored or overwhelmed, and how the involvement with the lesson grows rapidly with time.

Parents are our best sources for information about the child's life outside the studio. If Susan has just been to the zoo and has had an exhilarating but exhausting time there, we may need to make some adjustments in the progress of the lesson to accommodate her mood. Does Josh have a cold coming on? Family troubles, however minor, something special happening at school, excitement over an impending vacation or a visit from grandparents—all have an impact on lessons and you need to know about them. Telling parents that children may need a snack before lessons so that growling tummies won't demand attention is a useful practice. I often keep a bowl of healthful snacks on hand for such urgencies. That practice led to a new nickname—Mrs. Raisin.

At home   Parents need educating about the piano at home, and it can be a delicate subject. Piano lessons shouldn't be available only to middle-class children whose parents can afford a relatively costly instrument, but often that is the practical reality. Even with the best intentions, the situation in which a child has access to a piano at Grandma's, at a neighbor's, or at a community center simply doesn't work well. Many piano teachers hope for the day when some sort of scholarship system will allow every family with the desire to give this wonderful gift to their children.

However much you empathize with financial constraints, you can feel confident encouraging parents to purchase the best instrument they can afford. A superior instrument graces the efforts of the child and the whole family and this should be explained.

Occasionally, pianos can be "rented to own," and you often can help families find good used instruments through your community networks. Sometimes parents may worry that the instrument will end up being an expensive relic if the child gives up piano. Few children abandon the piano, however, and those who do may return to it. I've rarely known a case in which a piano was purchased only to be surrendered later. Parents need to know, as well, that the visit from the piano tuner isn't the time to show the young child from the room. Watching the tuner can be an enriching experience for everyone.

Location of the piano is very important. Parents eager to provide their young musician with every opportunity for concentration may be inclined to place the piano in a basement family room or other quiet, isolated place. Let them know that the piano should occupy a place of pride in the home, and that the flow of natural family traffic around the instrument is desirable. Children don't want to be alone or separated from the life of the family while they play. If they are, how will their naturally exuberant desire to "show off" their growing skills be encouraged? You should assure parents that a child's playing can be a happy accompaniment to preparing meals or other work around the home. Parents often mention that their children are drawn to touch the piano, even for a moment, whenever they pass through the room—they just cannot resist playing. This is, of course, the idea.

Besides the piano, parents sometimes ask if there are other musical toys and play instruments they can offer their young children (and their children's siblings) to help encourage a musical milieu. The toy store shelves are filled with a veritable orchestra of instruments, most of which offer more in the way of imaginative play than musical learning. But there are lovely sounding tubular bells pitched to a scale and bells arranged in a circle that can provide a certain amount of learning and listening fun. Good quality toy xylophones are nice to have at home and in the studio. They may not be perfectly in tune, but most of them closely approximate the sound of the scale. Music boxes can be fun, too.

If possible, each child should have his or her own music *machine*. Once, this was a turntable and records, an anachronism in these days of compact discs! Encourage parents to invest in inexpensive tape players as gifts for their children. They often become the most used objects of childhood. Making recordings of the children playing in the studio (see chapter 7) provides them with an audio record of their progress. Years later, they delight in playing the tapes of their first sounds, just as they delight in seeing movies of themselves taking their first steps.

Of course, the piano is the greatest musical toy of all.

Beyond the piano and recorded music, you can encourage parents to expose their children to music performance in all its varieties. Even a two-year-old can experience the enjoyment of a concert, although, as common sense dictates, certainly not two solid hours of chamber music.

Short visits, however, to school or community concerts in casual environments, choirs at church, family "sock hops" in the living room—all of these can be wonderful opportunities. Attend the first half of a concert, followed by a trip to the ice cream parlor, and you've concocted an endearing memory for a young child, reinforcing the art habit in ordinary life at the same time.

Aesthetic appreciation that begins in earliest youth can continue through life in a seamless fabric. Even though the teacher has no direct influence on offering a broad musical base at home, we can point out that the art habit has a way of rippling through a family. Older siblings may sometimes join in performing with the new student, and younger siblings who hear a brother or sister play may be encouraged to play themselves when they are old enough. Father may pull his guitar out of the closet where he's stored it since college days. Mother may remember a duet she played with her sister as a girl. Expertise is less important than joy—than the parents' positive response toward music. That love is communicated naturally.

Parents often are also concerned about their role in practice at home. You can assure them that they need not break out the stopwatch and enforce a rigid half-hour of practice at a certain time every day. If the piano is part of the child's home and life, the desire to sit down and play each day, even if just for a few minutes, will grow naturally, and may require only the gentlest reminder or none at all. Suggesting a regular practice period is helpful.

Though parents often are pleasantly surprised by the scope and depth of their child's repertory, you need to emphasize that repertory is not the goal; artistry is. Any time a

child sits down at the piano, that child is doing well and deserves praise from parents. You can encourage parents to give their highest praise to the child's attitude toward and involvement with the instrument rather than to her skill at executing any particular song. In the earliest years, most of the child's piano playing will be done during the framework of lessons. Playing at home should be a healthy, stress-free habit, an opportunity for private enjoyment or family performance. Children usually will be proud of what they're learning and more than willing to share it with the family.

Establishing communication _____

Parents want to talk about how their child is doing. It is important to take advantage of the opportunity to listen to their observations and concerns. But the moments after the lesson, with the child present and often impatient to get on with the day, are not usually the best time for sharing with parents. Give parents generous permission to phone you at home. Let them know the best times to reach you and assure them that if you are busy or unavailable, you'll welcome the opportunity to talk at another time.

Parents sometimes hesitate to "bother" the teacher at home by speaking to him or her by telephone. Try to dispel this concern, because a full and mutually supportive atmosphere of communication between parents and teacher is the best reinforcement a young student can have.

CHAPTER 5

The Teacher

One of the most obvious facts about grown-ups to a child is that they have forgotten what it is like to be a child.
    —Randall Jarrell

No magic recipe exists for teaching piano to the young child. Rather, there are techniques that any qualified teacher of piano already knows or can learn, and there are human qualities that are as important as musical or instructional skills.

Perhaps the most essential quality is liking children. It's not as simple as it sounds. We all like children; we like our own children and grandchildren and our friends' children. Liking children in a pedagogical context means more than liking their company. It means reaching inside to find the child within ourselves. Can we, while learning games in the studio, really share the children's enjoyment, beyond appreciating their fun? Can we set aside our own timetable, slow down, and allow the child to lead? Do we have patience, and by this I mean not a long-suffering willingness to put up with inappropriate behavior, but the true patience that comes when we see every child as an individual and every moment of every lesson as new?

Qualities of a capable teacher

A capable teacher of piano for young children should have the following qualities:

- Superior musicianship
- Respect for the child
- Flexibility
- Discipline
- Patience
- Humor
- Desire to empower
- Affection
- Lifelong commitment to learning

Superior musicianship   Early childhood years are foundation years. The learning that takes place during those years is never erased. It goes without saying that a teacher who is instructing young chil-

dren has the responsibility to strive for the highest possible standard of musicianship. The function of the teacher as role model cannot be overestimated. Your performances in the studio should be approached with as much seriousness as the ones in which you perform for adults.

The way you play, the joy with which you play, will be soaked up and emulated by your young students. And they will correct you, too, pointing out, for example, that you aren't facing the keyboard in the correct way. These are the moments when you find out just how fully they have incorporated the habit of piano playing.

Respect Respect for the child underscores your ability to see children as complete, important human beings. They learn from you and they teach you. But more important, you must always keep in mind that it's not the subject the child is interested in. It is you, the teacher, who is the focus for the young piano student. This is why your gestures of respect are so important.

Perhaps one symbolic gesture of respect is your willingness to kneel to the child's level when the child enters the studio—to meet the child physically, eye to eye, not tower above. The elaborate courtesy you show to children in the studio (always suggesting rather than insisting, being careful to observe the rules of polite speech) may seem old-fashioned to parents or observers. But just as young children respond best to slow, soft speech, they need clear and straightforward demonstrations of your respect for them. Public television's Mr. Rogers exemplifies this truth.

One of the most powerful ways you can show your respect to your young students is the manner in which you conduct the lesson. Establish control through guidance, telling your students *how* to do things rather than merely telling them *what* to do.

Young children know when they are being patronized. By the ages of three or four, a child wants to be addressed as an intelligent, affectionate human being. The child knows when he or she is doing well; he knows when he is having problems. If you are sure of yourself, children will trust you. Honesty should be your standard. If you are being honest emotionally with children, they will sense it, and they will return your respect.

Flexibility   There are no typical lessons and no typical children. The skillful teacher is a master tailor, crafting each lesson to suit the particular need of the child he or she is with at that moment. Also keep in mind the season, the weather, and the events of the particular week. Remember at all times that you are teaching a person, not just curriculum, and it is up to the child, with your guidance and inspiration, to absorb and use what he or she can.

An important test of our flexibility occurs when lesson plans go awry. There is that temptation to throw up our hands when the lesson seems to lag or when children are full of high spirits. That's when the knack for seeing musical opportunities in the most inopportune settings becomes critical. Children may remember for life the time you created a "sleepy song" for sleepy people on a day when everyone seemed tired, while what you had planned for that day may never have created such a lasting impression.

As a teacher, you need to keep your short-term and long-range goals foremost in your mind as you work. While it's important to have a general framework or plan for each lesson, you should also be alert to a child's expression of interest in a particular aspect of a lesson. Bird sounds in the piano? Where can we go with it? Does the sound of striking the tuning fork light up a young face? Perhaps matching the pitch on the piano can be an important discovery. The sound of music always comes first. The basic musical instinct, the simple awareness of pitch and rhythm, is our guide and standard. All else will follow.

The teacher is the guide, and it is critical to know, every day, where the expedition is headed, that is, how each step builds overall musical growth. And yet, the overriding goal is not the accomplishment of each and every step, but the feeling of accomplishment the child takes away from each lesson.

Discipline   This term is most often used in the context of childhood misbehavior. But in a piano lesson, which is a relatively brief period chock-full of experiences and joyous tasks, you should seldom be called on to discipline a child's outbursts or lack of attention. It has happened to me, but only rarely, and then for a specific reason relating to a specific child. I have found that gently asking the child to leave the studio, for a brief time or for the whole lesson, accomplished the purpose of restoring order and made the necessary impression on the student.

Patience   The temptation to rush ahead with a child who is just flying along, grasping concepts almost faster than you can teach them, is strong. Your objective, however, is not superficial attainment, but deep and lasting knowledge: proceeding slowly, building outward before you proceed onward, always varying your approaches so that the child always feels challenged.

Keep in mind the simplest principles:

- Show what you mean.
- Do first and explain later.
- Trust your instincts and your expertise.

Humor   Children are seeing the world new, and they are enormously captivated by its beauty and quirks. They know when adults are laughing at them and when their humor is being shared. Laughing along with children at the funny things they say does encourage them. So laugh along! Enjoy your jokes together. A period of "silliness" is very refreshing in the context of study and enhances, rather than detracts from, the learning process.

Humor also is a powerful pedagogical tool that makes it possible for children to respond positively to our suggestions and persuasions in ways that a too-solemn demeanor would not.

Desire to empower   A skillful teacher working with nursery school and early elementary school children should excise the word "don't" from his or her vocabulary and substitute the sentence "Let's try it this way." As teachers, we know that nothing builds self-esteem as well as encouragement and praise; nothing tears it down more quickly than negativity. This is not to say that you should not correct children's mistakes. In fact, children are hungry to do things well. But correction (helping a child to find a way to do something better) is distinct from destructive criticism, which attacks the person as well as the task.

In order to learn, children need the freedom to ask questions that may sound ridiculous and deserve a considered response to their question, not a put-down for asking it. When you allow mistakes and encourage risk-taking, you build artists who will dig deep into their creative resources. You build young people more likely to face the world with confidence, not fear.

Affection Good teachers like children and know how children respond to genuine, appropriate expressions of affection. A pat on the back, a clasp of the hand, a hug—all these help build the bond between teachers and students. Parents and children will be your best guide about what expressions of camaraderie and affection are most welcome.

Lifelong commitment to learning Just as you have committed to learning the special needs and characteristics of young children, you have adopted for yourself, as a teacher, the model of the constant scholar. Teachers of piano are always revising their high standards upward. We are always searching for techniques, refinements, new alternatives that can help young children learn.

Similarly, since the field of early childhood development is a frontier with rapidly expanding borders, you owe it to yourself and your students to keep current on the growing body of research from the fields of education and behavioral science that can help you better understand the way young children learn.

Teachers remain teachers only so long as they are in motion, growing year by year, in a constant process of discovery.

With the child, the parents, and the teacher, the three-legged stool of the piano experience is balanced and secure. In the next chapter, the basic principles of teaching piano to the young child grow naturally from an understanding of the way young children learn and from the capabilities of the teachers who guide them.

CHAPTER 6

Fundamental Teaching Principles

Example is the school of mankind, and they will learn at no other.
—Edmund Burke

As all music teachers know, we are teachers of human beings first, and of curriculum second. This perspective is critically important in working with young children. Our pedagogical objectives should be to lead our students to beautiful, graceful, knowledgeable playing, to a fluency in the language of music, and to a lifetime relationship with its beauties. But we are also working, along with parents and school teachers, to build powerful, confident individuals, secure in their abilities to tackle life's challenges and leap its hurdles.

The fundamental teaching principles

The fundamentals of teaching piano to young children can be outlined in ten basic principles, offered here as guidelines to forming your own educational plan.

- Let the relationship with the child come before the method.
- Let the sound of music come before anything else.
- Know your goals—both short- and long-range—and have a systematic way to review progress.
- Always show what you mean.

- Demonstrate now and explain later (often a *year* later).
- Advance slowly.
- Deal with difficulties by isolating problems, correcting them, then relating them to the total musical concept.
- Guide, suggest, and question your way to success.
- Keep the lesson simple, and always leave your students eager for more.
- Plan for success . . . and expect it.

Let the relationship with the child come before the method

From the way you bend to greet them as they enter the studio, to the questions you ask that make them feel important and interesting, your primary aim is always to show respect for your young students. Children who feel good about their teachers will feel good about what they're being taught. You can encourage this positive atmosphere in a number of simple but important ways.

The way you talk to children influences the way they feel about you. It is important to speak in a direct, friendly, and energetic way, letting the enthusiasm you feel for this work communicate itself to the child. The words you use can be simple and clear, but not affected or precious. Children may say and do silly things—so do adults—but they want to be taken seriously. So look into their eyes as you speak; really listen to them when they tell you things, without fidgeting inwardly to get on to the business at hand. This contact, this establishment of rapport, is fully as important to their musical study as their understanding of pitch and rhythm. Your communication should never be hurried or abrupt.

The way you move children through their lesson is based on this trust and familiarity. While you don't judge them or make unreasonable demands upon them, you do have high expectations. Experience with this kind of music teaching shows that the surest way to fulfill those expectations is to pack a lesson with many different activities children enjoy, then guide them with praise and encouragement toward accomplishing the tasks those activities encompass. Disruptive behavior arises from boredom and boredom is not a factor in a well-planned, well-timed lesson. The limits you set for children are positive limits, which you work toward together. You are able to guide them because you have something important to give them and because you love them.

Let the sound of music come before anything else

The first moments a child is in the studio are filled with the sound of music, with the hello song (see appendix 1, "Hello, Ev'rybody"), incorporating the child's name. Play it quickly or slowly, high or low, loud or soft on successive days, but be sure there is always the sound of music when they arrive and as they leave. The games and activities and, of course, the playing, all involve hearing and creating music.

Just as young children learn language first from the sound of it—before they ever realize that language is written down in symbols to represent the sounds—they learn music first from its beautiful sound. They can, in fact, learn to play music just from hearing it, though the study of music usually incorporates a more formal direction for that appreciation. Before they ever learn the term "staccato" young children know, with their minds and ears, how the short, bright sound differs from the lingering, resonant sound. The names come later, but they do come naturally, because the sound of music has opened the way.

Know your goals, both short- and long-range

Keep your long-range goals in mind as you construct the three elements of each lesson: listening, technique, and performance. Each challenge leads intimately into the next, and each, like streams feeding a river, moves the progression toward musicianship.

At a single lesson you might have such objectives as these:

- To teach keyboard geography, by approaching the immediate goal of discriminating between the "two black friends" and the "three black friends" (the black keys)
- To create an artist whose mind works through his or her hands, by teaching how arm staccato feels as opposed to wrist staccato
- To build performers, by arranging for half the time in the studio to be group experience

As a teacher of young children, you know that while you work within the framework of your goals, you focus on the child's pace, a pace that changes week to week, season to season. If you understand that any goal can be reached in at least a dozen different ways and that no one way is superior to another, you can free yourself from the pressures of seeing all learning as a linear path. An individual student may need, at a given time, to grow outward instead of upward, to work on improving his or her feeling of comfort in performance instead of progressing to more complex repertoire.

Preparing for piano parties is the most natural, direct review of progress. Piano parties, after all, are the focal points for performance in each year of lessons. Set forth plans to accomplish certain amounts of curriculum by certain dates or seasons, but within those goals should be a creative plan for each child, based on that child's temperament, interests, and progress.

Always show what you mean

Young children need to hear what they see and to see what they hear in the study of music. You should not attempt to *tell* your students what it means to play a phrase or a song "high" without *showing* them, simultaneously, what high means in musical terms. Amazingly soon, they begin to understand what the word—the symbol—means in musical terms. They "hear" with their developing musical ears what you have shown them. As they watch and listen, they learn almost without the conscious realization of the process. You are reaching the young child at a stage of life when much learning is sensory, and your methods of teaching can take ample advantage of that developmental reality.

Demonstrate now and explain later (often a year later)

Your students will be your best guide in determining how much explanation of any given element of the lesson they need. Give them only what they can use and try not to over-analyze. Too much explaining can defeat your purpose, actually leaving the young child puzzling intellectually over things that can be learned experientially. A good parallel is the growing practice among elementary school teachers of encouraging young students to write their ideas, feelings, and stories freely, without worrying about the grammar and spelling that can be "built in" as the child matures.

Advance slowly

Parents and teachers often are pleasantly surprised by the speed with which young children develop musical skills. However, teachers measure accomplishments, some of which are intangible, by many yardsticks. The evident satisfaction and attitude of the student are among the most important to me. Young children move ahead at rates that vary not only from child to child, but within each child's individ-

ual experience. A child will not metabolize all ideas at the same pace. Some assignments will progress slowly. Often, the child will gather momentum through a slower period and then spurt ahead. Realizing that there are no rules about how long it takes, you can look ahead with confidence.

Imagine that the goal is the sum of one dime. You begin with one penny, then another, then another—then suddenly a nickel, then three more pennies, in rapid sequence. It all adds up and you can take as much satisfaction in your students' variable ways of reaching their goals as you do in your many ways of guiding them.

Deal with difficulties by isolating problems, correcting them, then relating them to the total musical concept

We have already discussed the value of turning mistakes into positive experiences for young children by showing them immediately how correcting a problem makes the whole song or exercise work better. Isolate the problem while working on it, "Let's try it this way," then quickly relate that correction into the whole concept, "Now, come back and let's try it all together. Listen to how beautiful that sounds." This approach helps the child learn to view correcting mistakes as part of a process that makes a song sound better, rather than as occasions for distress.

Guide, suggest, and question your way to success

The knowledge students acquire by discovery and experience is more stable and enduring than knowledge acquired by "doing what you are told." With the young child, presenting alternatives, making suggestions, and guiding the way to problem solving is a surer path to success than issuing directives. Don't forget that you are partners in the study of music, not adversaries, and that there are many wonderful ways to achieve a desired result. Presenting acceptable alternatives and allowing the student to choose, even in matters as small as the color of marker used in the assignment book, give him a feeling of power. Your goal is to develop artists who know how to think and create, instead of technicians who know only how to repeat established patterns.

Keep the lesson simple and always leave your students eager for more

Experience shows us that sustaining enthusiasm over the long course is much more beneficial for the young child than subjecting him to a marathon. Lessons usually are no more than a half-hour in length, and at times your students will let you know that the lesson should be even shorter—that less is more. Children should always leave the lesson before they want to, so that they can return energized and eager in a few days. Students who feel that piano lessons are over too quickly are students fully engaged in the joy of music and they are a compliment to your sense of pedagogical timing.

Plan for success . . . and expect it

Come into a lesson "fat" and you will leave satisfied. Arrange each lesson not only to achieve specific goals, but to provide the maximum number of opportunities for success. (Expecting success is more than planning; it's a musical way of life.) Once you accept that a child basically cannot do wrong within the context of piano study, it is easier to approach the whole situation with a positive attitude. The student's desire to please combines happily with your desire to praise and empower. Viewing a lesson as a series of chances to succeed does not mean that you do not work hard and face significant challenges. For example, when you arrange for one child to follow another in an exercise or game, you must always be sure that the follower will be able to do what is asked. The *primary* challenge, however, is to do everything in such a "can do" atmosphere that children never doubt they are headed inevitably toward triumph.

With these principles in mind, we can move on to techniques and methods developed especially for teaching piano to the young child.

CHAPTER 7

Environment and Equipment

Do not try to satisfy your vanity by teaching a great many things. Awaken people's curiosity. It is enough to open minds; do not overload them. Put there just a spark. If there is some good inflammable stuff, it will catch fire.
—*Anatole France*

The space in which you work with the young child is the physical expression of your philosophy. As a teacher, you should attempt to let the surroundings reflect the joy and importance of the work that takes place there. The suggestions for arrangements included here are a basic guide, not a definitive plan. Creativity, inventiveness, and atmosphere are more important than specific materials or prescribed designs.

The environment

An in-home studio offers an excellent teaching environment and is usually a good alternative to a conservatory or music school studio. Ideally, the in-home studio and waiting room should be separate from the rest of the home or working area, although it need not be on a separate level. Effective arrangements are possible using screens or portable partitions to divide the studio from the waiting area and from the living space of the teacher's home.

The entrance can include space for hanging coats and other outerwear. The children's coat hooks work best if set at their level, so that they can "do it themselves." A large basket to hold the children's soft slippers or slipper-socks is also

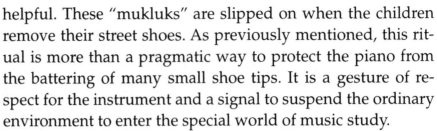

helpful. These "mukluks" are slipped on when the children remove their street shoes. As previously mentioned, this ritual is more than a pragmatic way to protect the piano from the battering of many small shoe tips. It is a gesture of respect for the instrument and a signal to suspend the ordinary environment to enter the special world of music study.

For the waiting rooms and studio, light, color, and visual interest are the keys. The waiting area might include posters and pictures with musical themes, as well as books, some on subjects that pertain to music. A low table and chairs for drawing and boxes of blocks and other safe toys help keep waiting students and young siblings busy. The waiting area should also provide comfortable seating for parents, reading material, a telephone, and a restroom, if possible.

The studio itself is a place that inspires excitement and endeavor. Many teachers worry that their space is too small, but this is usually not a problem. While the space should be large enough for movement and activity away from the piano, a relatively small space can enhance the closeness and intimacy of the teacher-student interaction. Similarly, though some teachers wonder whether they need two pianos, a single, well-tuned instrument emphasizes closeness. Sharing the space in front of one keyboard allows the teacher to manage and focus the child's energy and provides opportunities for encouragement through proximity and touch. Cushions and telephone books can be used to help students achieve the appropriate position, as can revolving stools that can be raised and lowered to accommodate the children's heights. Pedal extenders, available from piano tuners or music-supply dealers, are other useful tools.

Furnish the studio with the best lighting possible. Good lighting enhances both mood and visibility of the children's faces and the printed music. A lamp on the piano helps avoid shadows.

Another sensible purchase is small-sized chairs for the children that allow them to sit with their feet touching the floor. Since lessons involve standing, sitting, and moving around, often in brisk sequence, light, armless chairs work best.

Some of the teaching tools I have found most helpful in working with the young child are listed below, along with a short explanation of the use of each of the tools. You can begin working with the young child even though you haven't accumulated a full complement of such equipment. Some items obviously are essential, but others can be gradually acquired. In fact, many objects you already have in your home or studio may be adapted for use with young children.

Materials and equipment

The Teacher Provides

- The piano
- Printed music
- Cardboard keyboards
- Beanbags and balls
- Pipe cleaners
- Checkers
- Vanilla wafers, pretzel sticks, and lollipops
- Musical flash cards
- Magnetic board and magnetized musical notes
- Conductors' batons or other light, smooth sticks
- Blindfolds
- Cotton balls (with small boxes to put them in) and toy trucks or cars
- Scarves
- Drums, rhythm sticks, and other percussion instruments
- Cuisenaire Rods
- Wide-spaced music manuscript books
- Large newsprint pads, colored construction paper, small note pads, and colored markers or pens
- A metronome
- Floor mats
- An instant (Polaroid-type) camera
- A tape recorder
- Premoistened towelettes
- Snacks and treats
- A telephone and answering machine (optional)

The Student's Family Provides

- Audio- and videotapes (blank)
- Studio slippers
- Carry bag for music materials

The teacher provides First, let us consider what the teacher provides:

The Piano Whether it is a grand, an upright, a studio upright, or console, the piano is the soul of the studio. Inviting a piano tuner to give a minilecture on the way the instrument actually works (and how it looks inside) can foster an understanding of the piano's complexity and importance for the children. Keeping the instrument polished also reinforces its status. Offering premoistened towelettes to cleanse young fingers before students approach the keyboard communicates respect for the instrument.

Printed Music It is best for the teacher to select, purchase, and provide the printed music, so everyone can be assured of having the books when they are needed. The children I teach have many different books of music because I believe there are many different avenues to reaching the desired goal.

Cardboard Keyboards Write the letter names of the notes on cardboard keyboards and place them along the end board above the actual keyboard to help beginners *see* the sounds they hear.

Beanbags and Balls Children learn with their bodies as well as with their minds. Using beanbags and balls for rhythmic training that involves tossing, lifting, and other movement is both vivid and safe.

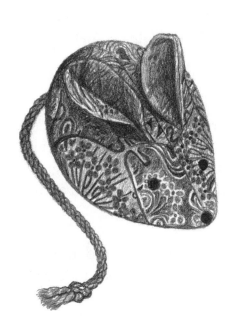

Find soft plastic balls about 13 inches in diameter (about the size of a volleyball) for this purpose and choose beanbags in bright colors and patterns.

Pipe Cleaners The children use pipe cleaners to design and construct music notes and clefs. The pipe cleaners can also be used to arrange rhythmic patterns.

Checkers Checkers can symbolize the notes on a staff that the teacher draws on newsprint—red for the space notes and black for the line notes.

Vanilla Wafers, Pretzel Sticks, and Lollipops Vanilla wafers also can represent notes on a staff drawn on newsprint by the teacher. Later, pretzel sticks are added to represent stems. Lollipops, with their "stems" already attached, come last. (Children take this edible "music" home after class.)

Musical Flash Cards The teacher holds up musical flash cards and asks the child to tap out or play the patterns in ear-training exercises. Many kinds of cards are available, offering varied approaches to core ideas.

Magnetic Board and Magnetized Musical Notes These boards have the advantage of being neat and easy to use, and they can be used again and again. Magnetism is one of the favorite mysteries of childhood, and using these boards makes the visual symbols of music compelling in yet another way.

Conductors' Batons or Other Light, Smooth Sticks   Students can conduct at the very beginning, in 2/4 time. There is a great sense of control in knowing that the other students (at the piano or playing rhythm instruments) must wait until the conductor signals the downbeat to begin. The students in the "orchestra" learn to focus on the conductor and work in concert.

Blindfolds   The blindfold, which should be brightly colored and attractive, allows children to experience the keyboard kinesthetically. Ask them, for example, to find two or three black keys with their hands, feeling the way. The blindfold also encourages them to experience the sounds they make with their hearing focused without any visual distractions. Be sure to gauge the way each child feels about having his or her eyes covered before making the attempt. I find that putting a blindfold on myself first tends to build a child's confidence.

Cotton Balls (with a small box to put them in) and Toy Trucks or Cars   All of these tools can help teach correct placement of the hands and fingers on the keyboard. Children make little "tunnels" of their hands that the tiny truck or car can drive through (allow them to choose the fantasy "destination," be it Grandma's, Disney World, or Timbuktu). They can hold the cotton balls in their palms as if they were fragile blossoms or snowflakes, which they must not crush, and they should be reminded to maintain the proper hand position even when the "snowflake" is removed. The correct finger position comes out of this naturally.

Variations: In spring and summer, ask the child to imagine she is holding make-believe flowers in a curved hand. "Make sure you hold them carefully so the flowers won't get crushed."

In winter, ask the child to pretend she is holding a soft snowball that can't be squashed.

Also, throw out paper tissue onto a table and ask the child to pick it up by extending her hand and scooping the tissue up into the palm.

Students can take their cotton balls for hand positioning at home.

Scarves Bright scarves of many sizes are useful for all manner of movement to music. They're especially well suited for Dalcroze eurhythmics (see p. 69 and Bibliography for more information) and other movement exercises. Giving children a choice of beautifully colored scarves heightens their enjoyment.

Drums, Rhythm Sticks, and Other Percussion Instruments Seek out the best-sounding drums and other instruments you can find. Sanded and cut to about 10 inches in length, rhythm sticks are a good tool for tapping out rhythms children hear and are asked to replicate. They also can be used for rhythmic accompaniment and games.

Cuisenaire Rods These small, brightly colored wood or plastic rods, originally used for teaching mathematical concepts, can make rhythm and melody tangible realities for children, without the need to write. The rods are graduated in size, with a given color corresponding to each size, and they come in a series from 1 to 10 (for music study, we use 1 to 8, to represent the octave).

Working with Cuisenaire Rods helps visually to teach changes in pitch. The child can create a "staircase" to learn ascending or descending melodic patterns. I have found it useful to remove one of the rods in the "staircase" after asking the children to listen to the pattern of five notes, then eight notes. The children can then be asked to sing the pitch they don't see. Eventually, the children can do all of this themselves. In addition, the varying sizes of the rods make rhythm demonstrable to the youngest child, and they can be used later to "construct" melodies—an early form of melodic notation.

Wide-spaced Music Manuscript Books A wide-spaced music manuscript notebook is presented and inscribed with the child's name at the first lesson and is needed throughout the year for weekly assignments. Each assignment is written in a different color.

Large Newsprint Pads, Colored Construction Paper, Small Note Pads, and Colored Markers This equipment is used for "drawing to music." For example, the children can draw a long, vertical line for strong beats and a shorter one for weak beats. Washable markers or pens are best when working with the young child.

A Metronome A metronome can dramatize specific exercises.

Floor Mats Small floor mats are useful to establish the child's individual territory or island for group lessons.

An Instant (Polaroid-type) Camera Children have their photo taken and displayed at their very first lesson. With this ceremony of initiation, they join the ranks of the other students whose pictures are displayed on the studio wall; it's a meaningful feeling of inclusion. I have used a standard camera for taking the photos, but waiting to have the film developed spoiled the immediacy of the ritual. Since Polaroid-type cameras are now inexpensive and readily available, investing in one is a good choice.

A Tape Recorder Record each student's work when special pieces are played and keep copies as an archive for the entire course of the child's study, to be returned when the child "graduates."

Premoistened Towelettes Hand or travel "wipes" are used by the students for cleansing hands before playing. "Baby wipes" don't work as well. They contain lanolin, which can make the hands slippery.

Snacks and Treats I like to provide lollipops, raisins, or some other safe and nonmessy snack to my students and their siblings. Snacks help head off hunger and can serve as gestures of friendship and rewards for a job well done.

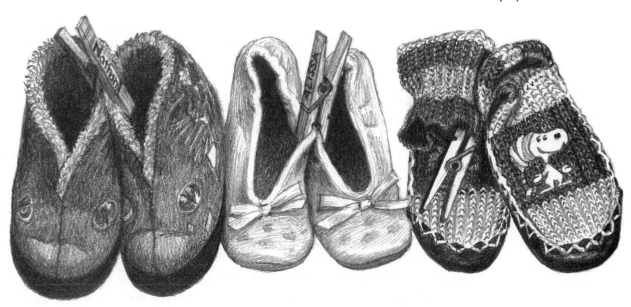

A Telephone and Answering Machine (optional)

Parents of young children often need access to a telephone. Providing one is an important and appreciated courtesy. It need not be a separate line. The answering machine, while not essential, can be useful for messages and helps avoid interruptions during lessons.

The family provides

Here is what the parents should provide:

Student Audio- and Videotapes (blank)

When lessons begin, parents provide blank cassette tapes on which children record some of their most memorable performances throughout the school year. Students introduce these performances, and many of my "graduates" have told me how they treasure hearing again their voices from earlier years announcing their first songs. I have also found it useful to make video recordings of piano parties and other performances for the children to see and hear at a later time. Video equipment is expensive, but it can be rented or borrowed for special occasions at a reasonable cost. Parents often enjoy obtaining copies of the videotapes of piano parties as cherished keepsakes.

Studio Slippers

Parents provide a pair of slipper-socks or other soft shoes for the studio which remain in the studio for the entire school year rather than being transported each time from home. Putting on your music shoes not only is a useful psychological tool for the transition from school or play to music study, it also allows greater ease of movement in class.

Carry Bags for Music Materials   Each child needs a carryall bag he or she can manage alone to carry home assignments, printed music, and other materials.

Sources for equipment and supplies

School supply stores, discount stores, catalogues, and music stores are the best resources for such equipment as small tables and chairs, magnetized musical notes, flash cards, balls, beanbags, percussion instruments, and paper products. Library and school book sales are a good source of books for the waiting areas, and safe toys in good shape often turn up at neighborhood garage sales. Scarves usually come from teachers' or relatives' wardrobes of fashions past, and families of students sometimes are kind enough to donate them.

(See Bibliography and References for information on teaching materials, including addresses for Dalcroze and Cuisenaire information.)

CHAPTER 8

Teaching Strategies— Keyboard Geography and Ear-Training

What we have to learn to do, we learn by doing.
—Aristotle

Young children are more interested in their teachers than in the subjects being taught. You are the focus for the child, so the way you teach—including varying the cadence and intensity of your voice in order to capture the child's interest or to emphasize the points you are making at the piano—is as important as the material. Techniques and methods of teaching piano targeted specifically at the young child can build a sense of fun and closeness that assists learning. Always remember that children accomplish specific tasks at different rates. One child may grasp a concept almost instantly, but may need several lessons to learn another, even if the second is closely related to the first. Give the child many chances for success, always demonstrating a skill one last time before asking him to perform it for you.

The wide range of learning activities described here is intended to help teachers approach the basic material in many different ways, so that each child gets many opportunities to learn each concept. There is no one correct way to absorb knowledge. Find what works well, whatever it is, and embrace it.

Fun and activity are the bywords. Children learn most durably what they experience, so create opportunities to let them use their bodies and get to the keyboard as often as possible. Vary activities frequently during the lesson, trying something new every two to three minutes. For the children, studio time should never seem long enough. Though children are aware only of the enjoyment and the pleasure of beautiful sound, they are actually absorbing by activity musical principles that would be too complex to explain to them.

Along with describing the use and purpose of the assignment book, we will concentrate in this and later chapters on methods for teaching:

- Keyboard geography
- Ear-training
- Rhythm
- Music reading
- Technique
- Finger games
- Fundamentals of performance

Keyboard geography

The keyboard is a new world to children, and we guide them by demonstrating from the first moments of the lesson what "high" and "low," "top" and "bottom," and "up" and "down" mean in the world of piano.

The *concepts* to be established in learning *keyboard geography* are:

- The piano keyboard has patterns that correspond with locations.
- The piano keyboard has patterns of black notes in twos and threes.
- The piano keyboard has a top, a middle, and a bottom, with sounds that correspond to those locations.
- The piano keyboard begins at the lower left end with "A."
- The piano keyboard is made up of notes with letter names in repeated patterns going upward.

The *skills* to be mastered are:

- Finding and playing the two black and three black friends.
- Understanding the patterns of the two and three black friends.
- Learning the difference between "high" and "low" (up, down; top, bottom) in "keyboard-ese."
- Learning the letter names of the notes and how to find them.
- Learning to find and play the notes by hearing their letter names.
- Learning the names and meanings of sharps, flats, and naturals.

The activities you can use to help children with keyboard geography are:

Two Black Friends and Three Black Friends

- Show the black note twos and threes.
- Explain that they are "friends" because they are side by side.
- Reinforce the idea of "two" by asking the child to hold up two fingers on one hand (most three-year-olds can do this).
- Repeat with the other hand, then ask the child to hold up three fingers.
- Now ask the child to find the two black friends up and down the keyboard. Then ask him to find the three black friends.
- Have the child stand at the piano—for a young child, standing is the easiest position from which to negotiate the entire keyboard, not only the area around middle C. (They also will want to sit, since they associate sitting at a keyboard with how adults or older students play. From the beginning, be sure to give them opportunities to play sitting down as well.)
- Ask the child to find the two black friends again.
- Suggest, "Let's play them high. Let's play them low."
- Ask the child to play the two (then the three) black

friends high, low, and in the middle. Play them loudly and softly.

- Demonstrate "Hot Cross Buns," on the highest of the three black notes, putting the child's hands over yours as you play.
- Next, ask her to try it alone.

It is very important that each child leave the very first lesson playing something. Many will be able to play at least the first three notes of "Hot Cross Buns" (see p. 95) at the beginning lesson, or "Baby Bunnies" (see appendix 3).

Meet the Music Alphabet

- Place a cardboard keyboard behind the keys. Adjust the cardboard so that the first note on the lower left is A.
- Tell children that A is the lowest note on the piano and that all the other notes go up from that note in a musical alphabet.

It takes time to understand that the letters go up from A to G and then start over again with A. We simply repeat it over and over, not explaining. The concept becomes solidified through the repetition.

- Point to any note anywhere on the piano and ask the child what it is. Most won't know.
- Then suggest the way to find out, by "counting up" from the lowest A to G, over and over until we reach it.

With the youngest children, the idea of alphabet progression may not be as fixed, and it is not as urgent for them to learn the letter names as quickly. The youngest children can fly about on the keyboard with only the knowledge of the location of the two and three black friends. Age appropriateness and experience with letters are your guides here.

Hi Diddle Diddle, the D's in the Middle

- Most children, from three on up, are able almost at once to find the two black friends.
- As the child points to the two black friends, repeat, "Hi

diddle diddle, the D's in the middle." The D is in the middle of the two black friends.

- Over the course of a few lessons, ask the child to find all the high Ds and all the low Ds.
- When that concept is secure, ask, "What comes after D?" He'll know that E comes after D. Ask him to play E.
- Next, have him play D and E (a "step up"). Play the D/Es all over the piano. When playing this "step up" is secure, try stepping down, E to D.
- To teach C, recite the alphabet. C comes before D, E, which the child knows by then.
- By the time we add F and G, we have the first five tones of the major scale. Be sure to add B and A last; A tends to be a more difficult note to find, unlike middle C. By the time the child can play ABCDEFG, the child knows the letter names and can locate them all over the keyboard.

Ear-training

In *ear-training*, the *basic concepts* to be mastered are these:

- Music can be fast, slow, high, low, loud, or soft.
- Music can have melodies that move up or down by steps.
- Music can have melodies that move up or down by skips.

The *skills* involved are these:

- Stepping up and stepping down.
- Recognizing repetition and patterns.
- Beginning notation.
- Listening for sounds to reproduce them.
- Recognizing major and minor keys.
- Beginning transposition and improvisation.

The hello song (high, low, etc.) The sound of music comes first. At the lesson, children begin experiencing the sound of music from the moment they are greeted by the "hello" song ("Hello, Ev'rybody" by Charity Bailey, see appendix 1). The hello song is the cornerstone for teaching the differentiation between HIGH and LOW on the keyboard. Children may think that the "high" point of the piano refers to the lid of the cabinet, that the "low" point refers to the pedals. Using different ways of playing the hello song at each lesson, you can demonstrate that these are terms for sound, not just location.

- Play the greeting song high.
- Indicate, at the same time, what "high" means in keyboard-ese.
- Repeat showing the child that the "top" of the keyboard contains notes that are "high," notes that are "up" on the piano.
- Next time, play the song through in the middle of the keyboard first.
- Then ask, "Shall I play it high this time, like this?" Repeat the terms that "mean" the sounds, using "high," "top," and "up" interchangeably during successive lessons.
- Use the same principle to demonstrate the other half of the sound pairs, "low," "bottom," and "down" of the keyboard.
- Ask, "Shall I play this high?" (Your voice goes high.) "Or low?" (Your voice drops low.)
- Bring the child to the piano to try to place his hands over yours as you play.
- Teach concepts of FAST/SLOW and LOUD/SOFT in the same way.
- Play any song, letting the child choose which variation to hear. (Most want to hear songs played loud, fast, and high.)
- Then play the opposite of the variation, asking the child to listen for the differences.
- Play a song and then hum it with the child.
- Next, ask the child to clap it out.
- Begin by clapping slowly.
- Next time through, add slow singing.
- Invite the child to get up and walk slowly as you play slowly, then add slow clapping to the slow walking.
- Repeat with fast clapping, singing, and running.

Sunflowers
- Ask the child to imagine that she is in a garden planting sunflower seeds.
- Play the first five tones of the major scale and ask the child to imagine the sunflowers are growing: "RISE . . . UP . . . TO . . . THE . . . SUN!" (The child stretches up tall.)
- Then, as you descend the scale, "DROP . . . DOWN . . . ONE . . . BY . . . ONE!"
- Move her one step to the right or left (the next "row" of flowers) to go up a half step chromatically to C sharp, then to D, etc.).

The ladybug   The ladybug is a good image to use in teaching young children because it is a small, friendly creature familiar to most of them. In fact, this image is a powerful tool, with many applications.

- Ask the child to listen to the ladybug going up a blade of grass (first five tones of the major scale).
- After you play the note once, invite the child to play what he heard.
- Repeat until the child is comfortable with the sounds and the feel of the sounds.
- Now ask the seated child to imagine that he is the blades of grass.
- On the sound of the first tone, the ladybug is "on" his toes. He touches his toes.
- At the second tone, the ladybug is at his knees, then his tummy, then his shoulders, and finally, his head. He has divided his body into five tones.

It may take several sessions for the child to be comfortable with the progress up the scale. Once it is established, the ladybug can begin to walk down.

- At another lesson, begin the five-note pattern with another note.
- Point out that the ladybug can start from each of the twelve tones.

- After moving up-1-2-3-4-5-ask if the ladybug would like to skip down-5-3-1 (head, tummy, toes).
- Or, ask if the ladybug can jump 5-1 (head to toes).
- In successive lessons, ask the child to listen for the moment when the ladybug skips a note.
- As the child develops the ability to play five-note patterns, let him or her be the teacher, asking you and the others to listen for the moment when the ladybug skips a note. This approach can be used with the Cuisenaire Rods.

Birds in the corner Since young children want to move and need to change position often, you might have better success asking them to listen actively, rather than to sit quietly in a chair to listen. Focused listening should be an important part of every lesson.

- Ask the child to pretend to be a little bird, finding a comfortable corner in the room to roost and listen.
- Allow her to choose whether she wants to be a robin, a bluebird, or the swan she saw at the zoo.
- Ask her to close her eyes and focus on the music you play for her—usually simple songs with words at the beginning, since the sound of words establishes the rhythmic and cadence sense of the early music experience. Choose nursery songs, "Hot Cross Buns" (see p. 95) or "Baby Bunnies" (see appendix 2), for the first efforts.
- Ask the child to listen first, then sing the song once again.
- Then ask the child to come to the piano, putting her hands on top of yours as you play.
- Finally, give the child the chance to play what she has heard. Some children may play only the first two phrases; some the whole song. It doesn't matter whether it takes three lessons or three months to repeat the sounds. Have them set their own pace.

Melody writers Young children can begin taking melodic dictation almost immediately, using their fingers, the Cuisenaire Rods, and other objects as their tools, long before they can write.

- Play the first five tones of the major scale, up and down.

- Ask the child to assign, with her hand, different heights for each of the notes. Then have her move her hand accordingly with each note.
- At another lesson, use Cuisenaire Rods to "build" the first five tones of the major scale. The smallest rod is the white, for the first note, the red, green, purple, and yellow rods follow.
- Point to them as you play.
- Bring the child immediately to the piano to play the first five tones.
- Next, use your hand with the thumb on top and palm facing you, and open the fingers to represent a staff.
- Ask how many fingers are on one hand. These represent the lines of the staff.
- Then ask, "What's between the fingers?" (We hope that the answer will be "spaces.")

Note games
- Draw a large staff on newsprint. Five lines are sufficient and it is not necessary to draw a clef at first. (See figure below.)
- Number the lowest line "1," the next line "2," and so on.
- Draw circles to represent the notes on each line.
- Using black checkers, ask the child to place a black checker on line 1, line 2, and so on.

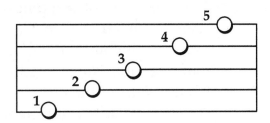

- Draw another staff.
- Number the spaces as you did the lines above.
- Using black checkers, ask the child to place the line notes, and use the red checkers to place the space notes.
- On another staff, use vanilla wafers instead of checkers.
- Give the child opportunities to practice putting the notes on the staff.
- After the vanilla wafers are understood, add straight sticks to represent the stems.

• Show the child that if the note is below the third line, the stem goes up on the right. If it's above the third line, the stem goes down on the left. (This is a more complex notion and takes most children more time to absorb. Present it again later.)

Lollipops (wrapped) with their "stems" already attached come last. And the young students are allowed to take home all the "notes" in a plastic bag at the end of the lesson to enjoy later as treats. Eventually, after they develop the hand control they need (few do before age five), children will be able to write the notes on the staff as you play.

Playing by ear is an enjoyable skill we as teachers can encourage from the beginning. Whatever children play— melodies they hear in TV commercials or themes from movies or symphonies—is a cause for celebration, since it means the ability to hear, absorb, and synthesize as their own. They may even want to play a thunderstorm they heard one night by remembering how it sounded.

Step and skip
• Use your two hands to form steps in the air or draw a group of steps on a pad of paper.
• Ask the child to "step up" with her fingers as you play C to D. That's a step. Move her to the piano to try it herself.
• Once the idea of stepping up is learned, demonstrate "step down," from C to B. (The reality that one is a whole step and the other a half step is a foreign concept to a four-year-old; associating the steps to the letter names is what counts for them.)
• After the child is comfortable with "step up" and "step down" (and, again, this will take varying lengths of time for each child), move on to skipping. Play CE for a skip up, then CA for a skip down. Do this from various tones.

Use the lollipops (or vanilla wafers and pretzel sticks) on the hand-drawn staff or the magnetic board with magnetized musical notes to reinforce skipping and stepping in another way. The whole idea will take more than a few lessons to grasp.

Harmonic changes   The ideas and methods of Emile Jacques-Dalcroze comprise a system of games and exercises to develop rhythmic unity among the mind, ear, eye, and body in order to express outwardly, by movement, the inner understanding of music. You can employ Dalcroze principles in many ways, one of which is teaching harmonic changes by asking children to walk to the sound of music played on the piano.

- Play any song (e.g., "Mary Had a Little Lamb") using only the tonic chord. This is, of course, incorrect, but it will draw the child's attention.
- Then play the same song, using the correct chord changes.
- Ask the child to listen for the changes.
- At the instant the chord changes occur, have the child change direction and listen for the music to change again. A simple exercise, but it can have a profound effect.

Spaces between sounds
- Start with the interval of the second (adjacent tones).
- Ask the child to listen first.
- Now ask the child to play, pointing out that this is the closest movement, sound, and letter we can make on the keyboard.
- Say, "This is step up," then hum it, then play it.
- After the child masters playing "step up" (the evidence is usually their ability to play it quickly), then repeat the process for "step down."
- Play a series of notes low, high, and in the middle.
- Ask each time, "Am I stepping up? Or stepping down?"
- Go up the octaves, playing all the Cs on the piano, starting at the low end.
- Ask the child, "How many Cs am I playing?"
- In later lessons, ask the child to listen for the time when the teacher "forgets" one of the Cs. "Which one is missing?" we ask, and in a surprisingly short time, the child will be able to answer, "The fifth one. You forgot the fifth one."

The majors and minors   Though the subject of major and minor tonality does not occur in the first years of lessons, one method for teaching a child to recognize the difference is to play a familiar song, such as "Mary Had a Little Lamb" or "Happy Birthday." First, play it the familiar way. Then change it to a minor key. Most children hear the difference instantly.

Moving the houses

- Use the familiar device of the "two black friends" and the "three black friends" to teach the idea that melodies can be played on different parts of the keyboard.
- Ask the child to find the two, then the three black friends on the keyboard and play them.
- Now point out that the friends are moving.
- Make it clear that when they move, everything that is in the house moves with them; it will be the same group of sounds, but in a different place.
- "Move the house," asking the children to play the two black friends all the way to the top of the keyboard, then all the way back down. Repeat with the three black friends.

The ladybug also is useful in early training in transposition. Start the ladybug going up in the key of C, then move to the next key, C♯, then D, and so forth.

Freestyle Improvisation is one of the children's favorite activities, and we can facilitate it by guiding them to play on the black keys only, because no matter what they play, it will sound beautiful.

- Decide together what kind of song the child would like (fast, slow, happy, sad, etc.).
- Name the song (e.g., "Walk in the Misty Woods").
- Then play a bass accompaniment on the black keys, setting the mood of the song. Use tone clusters, random notes, arpeggios, or chords.
- The child can then join in, playing any combination of black notes he desires.
- Try playing more softly to lead the child into changing the nature of the sound, then more loudly, then slower.
- When the song ends, stop and hold one long, last note.

Later, help the student make up a different idea for an improvisation, using a different mood, tempo, and the like: "At the Zoo," "Snow," "Swimming in the Lake," for example.

The freedom to "compose" beautiful sounds is a profound experience for the young child.

Repeat the musical sentence Every time they hear a phrase repeated, children are learning the sentence structure, the form of the music. From the simplest song, such as "Hot Cross Buns," they are experiencing phrases.

- Choose one child's name.
- Play the syllables (in notes) over and over in the same way: "Jim-my, Jim-my, Jim-my."
- Now move to a different part of the keyboard, asking, "Is this higher or lower?" As they listen, they begin to absorb the sequential nature of the music.

CHAPTER 9

Teaching Strategies—Rhythm and Reading

Music is the arithmetic of sounds as optics is the geometry of light.
—Claude Debussy

With rhythm training as with ear training, the sound of music comes first. Singing, clapping and dancing to music are the first ways children express musical instincts.

Rhythm concepts

The *concepts* to be mastered in developing *rhythm sense* are these:

- Music has a steady beat.
- Music has rhythmic patterns.

The *skills* to be mastered are:

- Recognizing strong beats and weak beats
- Duplicating rhythmic patterns in various ways
- Understanding the differences among rhythmic patterns
- Understanding meter

Breakfast beats   The following are examples of activities that teach these skills:

- Begin by asking the child, "What did you have for breakfast this morning?"
- No matter what the answer is (even M&Ms), your answer is, "That's why you're so strong today." Explain then that sounds also can be strong or weak.
- Ask the child to close his eyes and listen as you play a song. Then ask, "Are certain notes in the song strong? Are others weak?"
- Next, play the song quickly, then slowly, each time asking for the child's reaction. Ask him to stand up and move, quickly as you play quickly, slowly as you play slowly. Ask him to begin moving when the music begins and to stop when it stops.

Power clappers
- As you play a song, ask the familiar question, "Are some of the sounds stronger? Do they sound louder?"
- With a song played in 2/4 time, ask the child to clap only on the strong beat (always begin with 2/4 time, working gradually into 3/4 and 4/4 time).

Clap and cluck
- After clapping on the strong beats is established, ask the child to listen again, this time for the strong and weak beats.
- Then ask the child to "cluck" on each weak beat and clap on each strong beat. Accomplishing this takes several sessions for most students.

A toss-up This exercise is based on tossing balls to music, but the first balls to use are make-believe.

- Ask the child to imagine that she is tossing balls into the air as you play songs in 2/4 time.
- Toss the ball up on the strong beat.
- Next, bounce the imaginary ball on the strong beat.

Walk, skip, and hop Starting and stopping to changes in music are other ways of establishing rhythm sense.

- Begin by asking the children to hop, walk, or skip in a circle clockwise. (Demonstrate what clockwise means.)
- When the music stops, ask them to reverse their direction.

- When the music stops again, the children change direction again. In this way, they begin to understand the form of music with their bodies.

Roll over, Ludwig

- In a group lesson, ask the children to sit on the floor and roll a plastic ball to another child on the strong beat.
- Next, ask them to roll the ball or pass it around the circle until the music stops. Next time, move the ball in the opposite direction.
- Use beanbags and balloons as alternative objects to be passed to rhythmic patterns. Varying objects and textures helps capture and keep children's interest.

When the skill is well established in 2/4 time, move on to the same exercises in 3/4 time, then 4/4 time. For more information on ways to use balls in music training, read *Rhythm Games for Perception and Cognition* by Robert M. Abramson (see Bibliography).

A later variation is asking children to listen not just to music stopping and starting but changing in some other

way—and asking them to change direction when the music changes.

Stamping and marching to music also are useful rhythmic motions.

We've got rhythm
- Play or tap out a rhythmic pattern.
- Ask the children to tap on the strong beats, using percussion instruments or drums.
- Ask them to exchange instruments, or to close their eyes while you rearrange the instruments.
- Repeat the exercise, so that each child has the chance to handle all the rhythm instruments.
- Now, with the teacher at the piano and the children using the finger cymbals, blocks, drums, or rhythm sticks again, ask the children to clap or tap on all the beats.
- Next, ask them to tap on the strong beats only.
- Finally, ask them to tap on the strong beats and cluck on the weak beats.
- Ask some children to tap on the strong beats and others to tap on the weak beats.

The scarf game
- Ask each child to choose a colorful scarf (use soft fabric, in oblong or rectangular shapes). Ask the children to stand up.
- When the music begins, have them move the scarf in time to the music. Children quickly realize that waving slowly as you play slowly requires a different motion than waving very quickly.
- Next, ask two children to stand facing one another, each holding the scarf by two corners.
- As you play, the children slowly raise and lower the scarf.
- Next, they work together to decide which way to move the scarf side to side, beginning to negotiate the early principles of ensemble playing.

Drawing meter
- Provide each child with large newsprint pads or smaller pads they can hold.
- Ask the children to sit on the floor.
- Allow each child to choose a favorite marker color.
- As you play in 2/4 time, ask the children to draw a long,

vertical mark for the strong beat, a dot for the weak beat. Do the same for 3/4 and 4/4 time. When the drawing is completed, count all the strong beats:

2/4 |•|•|•|
3/4 |••|••|••|
4/4 |•••|•••|•••|

A variation, after you introduce 4/4 time, is drawing pine trees. The trunk is the strong beat, the three parts of the tree top are the weak beats. (See figure below.)

Conductors   Children love the power of conducting an "orchestra" (it can be made up only of the teacher and child or of the other children and the teacher, playing the piano and rhythm instruments).

- Provide the child with a conductor's baton or smooth stick.
- Demonstrate the way to make a downward stroke to cause the group to play the strong beat and how to sweep up to indicate the weak beat. (Don't be surprised if a student, enjoying the captive audience who must pay close attention, makes the class wait for the downbeat until he or she is good and ready.) Children prefer to conduct quickly in 2/4 time; conducting slowly is difficult for them because of the need for greater control.

Music reading

Though the skills are established simultaneously, music reading is a natural progression that grows along with the ability to navigate the keyboard and recognize the keys. In this as in every case, we use sounds before symbols.

The *concepts* to be mastered in *music reading* are:

- Music steps up and music steps down.
- Music has patterns that can be repeated.
- Music has notes that are played for different lengths of time.
- Music notes will tell you how long to hold them by their appearance.
- Music notes are signs that mean sounds on the keyboard.
- Music notes have different locations going up the staff.

The *skills* to be established are:

- Finding and identifying notes by letter names.
- Finding and identifying where notes belong on the staff.
- Being able to play patterns from written or printed music.
- Understanding the concept of one beat and two beat notes.
- Recognizing quarter notes, half notes, whole notes, quarter rests, half rests, and whole rests.
- Understanding and recognizing clefs.

Some activities that establish these skills and concepts follow.

Note games
- Using a hand-drawn staff, begin as before with the checkers.
- Move on, again, to the vanilla wafers, then add the pretzel sticks.
- Last, use the wrapped lollipops with "stems" attached.

Be sure to give the young child the opportunity to be "teacher." You, the teacher, take the child's place in his or her small chair. Such activities let the child feel empowered and help reinforce learning.

The man who was too big for his bed (the G clef) I tell a story callled "The Man Who Was Too Big for His Bed" to teach the location and appearance of the treble clef. Calling it the G clef rather than the treble clef works well because the child who is learning to read music can associate the clef with the G line on the staff. (By this method, the bass clef is, then, the F clef.)

• As you draw the clef (see diagram below) tell the story of (1) the man who was too big for his bed: "He (2) got out of bed and went *around* to his living room and then *out* onto the porch to get his newspaper. He (3) had to stop at the black line or he'd fall off his front porch! On the way back (4), he meets Mr. G." In this way, children begin to recognize the symbol, but also have established the landmark note G. A story isn't necessary for teaching the F clef, once the G clef is established. Draw it, paying attention to the dots above and below F.

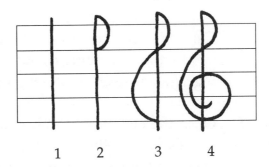

1   2   3   4

Look sharp   Other stories can be invented to describe the G clef, for example, "The Deer Who Walked Around the Pond."

• To introduce the child to "signs," play a familiar progression, such as the ladybug (the first five tones of the major scale).
• The second time, play one sound differently, for example, play C-D♯-EFG.
• Ask which note was different—one, two, three, four, or five.
• When the child answers that "2" was different, bring the child to the piano to show what made the sound different.
• Point out how we alter the sound.
• Show the child the sharp sign on a pad, on printed music, on a flash card.

Point out that a sharp sign (♯) before a note means to play the very next note higher. A flat sign (♭) in front of a note means to play the very next key lower. Tell them that sharps and flats are very powerful signs; just one in front of one note means that all those notes in that measure are "sharped" or "flatted" by that one sign.

- Point out that all notes have these different ways of being played (sharps and flats) and show where they are located.
- Ask the child to find and play C.
- Then ask the child to play C♯.
- Ask the child to play G. Then G♯.
- Then repeat the exercise with E. The child will say, "There is no E sharp!"
- Point out that the same sound can have different names. Play E, F, then E, E♯. F and E♯ are examples of enharmonic tones.

Use the same exercises for flats, first introducing a familiar sound, then changing it, but emphasize that flats mean moving down instead of moving up.

Looking for landmarks

Once the clefs are established and familiar to the children, you can place them on a hand-drawn grand staff to begin teaching them that in most cases notes that fall above middle C on the staff are in the G clef, and notes below middle C are in the F clef.

Begin showing children the symmetry and predictability of the staff by demonstrating that the grand staff is almost a mirror image of scales up and down.

- Starting with middle C, point out that two lines up is G (the G Clef) and two lines down is F (the F Clef).
- Up two spaces from the G is C again and two spaces down from the F is C again. Two ledger lines up above the G clef staff is C again. The combination of the easily found middle C and the clefs makes the symmetry clear.

Quarter notes, half notes, whole notes, and all the rests

Teaching the appearance, sound and value of notes is intimately related to ear-training.

- Begin by displaying the quarter note on the music stand or pointing it out in printed music, on a flash card, or as a magnetized note on the magnetic board.
- As you point out the quarter note, call it "one."
- Tell the children that whenever we see this note, we say "one."
- Practice clapping first one time, saying "one" as you do it.

- Show three quarter notes in a row.
- Clap them out, saying, "One, one, one."
- When quarter notes are established, repeat the procedure for half notes.
- Half notes are "two beat" notes.
- Ask the child to clap or play it this way: "One, hold." The child claps "one" and continues to clasp her hands together for "hold"; this physical symbol of "hold" transfers to the way the note is played on the piano. Both the "one" and the "hold" get a beat each.
- When this is firmly established, move on to the dotted half note ("One, hold, hold"). This is a "three beat note."

Using the words "one" and "hold" instead of the proper name may at first sound counterproductive. Yet, using the words "quarter, quarter," for example, detracts from the seamless symmetry between the sound, the sound of the verbal symbol, and the concept of the note's value. "Quarter" has too many syllables to be a "one" note, whereas the concept of "one" transfers very well to playing the notes on the piano.

It's important to begin with time, so be careful to purchase or edit all introductory music accordingly. Also, be sure that eighth notes, when you introduce them, appear only in pairs, as "partners," because the concept of two notes standing for one beat is too complex for the young child to master at first.

Teach rests in the same fashion, but use the word "off" or "rest" to represent the rest. (For example, a half rest is "off off" or "rest rest." Children can grasp that a rest in music means the same as a rest in everyday life, that is, a short period of silence.)

Editing the music   When you provide printed music for the beginner's lessons, make it music that has only five lines, not the entire grand staff. Use only the G clef at first.

After drawing the mitten (see next chapter, "Left and Right") to signify the right hand, edit the music as follows:

- Wherever the music steps up, draw a straight line to connect the notes (see 1, below).
- Wherever the music steps down, draw a straight line to connect the notes (see 2, below).
- Wherever the music skips down, draw a half-circle below the notes to connect the notes (see 3, below).
- Wherever the music skips up, draw a half-circle above the notes to connect the notes (see 4, below).
- Wherever two notes are the same, connect them with a wiggly line (see 5, below).

To indicate the note values on the printed music:

- Write "partners" for two eighth notes.
- Write a "1" for a quarter note.
- Write a "1h" (to mean "one, hold") for a half note.
- Write a "1hh" for a dotted half note.
- Write a "1hhh" for a whole note.
- At the end of the piece, write the word "off."

CHAPTER 10

Teaching Strategies— Technique and Performance

Fine art is that in which the hand, the head, and the heart of man go together.
  —John Ruskin

Technical development is an essential part of any plan for total musical growth at the piano. It is through technique that the young child puts into practice (into playing) all that he or she has learned.

Technique

Among the *concepts* involved in teaching *technique* are these:

- Music has many tones, moods, speeds, and variations.
- Music's beauty depends not only on knowing what notes to play but on how to play them.
- Music has signs that tell us whether it is to be played loudly or softly, quickly or slowly.

Among the *skills* to be mastered through learning *technique* are these:

- Understanding and developing staccato, legato, and sustained tones
- Developing musicianship through the art of phrasing

- Understanding differentiation and use of the five fingers
- Understanding dynamics: gradations from p through ff, as well as how moods are established through tonal variety
- Learning to play with the right hand, the left hand, and both hands

Left and right

- Sit on the bench to the right of the child.
- Begin by pointing out that "right" is the side where the teacher is sitting.
- Ask the child to find the middle of the keyboard (say that it's the place where the name of the piano is written).
- Point out that everything above the middle *usually* is right, and that "going up" *usually* means right.
- Point out that everything below the middle *usually* is left, and that "going down" *usually* means left.
- Ask the child what hand he or she uses to write or color.
- If it is the right hand, point out that this is "right."
- If it is the left hand, focus on the left hand and refer to the right hand as the "other hand." Keep your guidance and instructions focused on the hand the child favors for writing.
- On 3" × 5" cards, draw mittens (see figure below) with the thumb pointing right or left, using a red marker for the right hand, a blue marker for the left.

 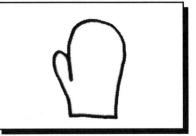

- (*Alternative*) Trace mittens onto different colored construction paper.
- Make piles of all the printed mittens, then mix them up.
- Ask the child to find all the mittens that are "lefts," then all the mittens that are "rights." He will accomplish this at first by looking at the colors and matching them.

- Next, make mittens the same color, on plain white paper, some with thumbs pointing to the left, some to the right.
- Mix them up and ask the child to find all the "rights" and all the "lefts." Now they must look for the difference in the way the thumb is pointing.
- Ask the child to raise his right hand.
- Ask the child to come to the piano and play something with his right hand (or left hand).
- Ask the child to "shake" his right hand.
- With a washable marker, label one hand "R," the other "L."
- Make a pipe cleaner "R" and a pipe cleaner "L" and attach these to the child's hands with rubber bands.
- When the child begins learning clefs, make a G clef from pipe cleaner for the right hand, an F clef for the left.
- When music reading begins, draw mittens on the page.
- If the child is to use the right hand, draw a mitten with the thumb pointing left, the reverse for the left hand.

Let's do wiggle-fingers   As they approach differentiating and numbering fingers, children need a number of different but related strategies to solidify a single concept.

- Ask the child to wiggle all her fingers.
- Wiggle your own fingers and show how to really get those fingers moving.
- Now ask the child to wiggle, in order, thumbs, pointers, middle fingers, fourth fingers, and smallest (fifth) fingers.
- Now ask the child to place the hands together, the heels of the hands pressed together and the tips of the fingers touching. (*Placing the hands together saves on explanation, and possible confusion, about why the fingers are numbered as they are.*)
- Number the fingers, with the thumb number 1, the pointer number 2, and so on.
- Repeat the finger-wiggling game, asking the child to wiggle number 1, 2, and so on.
- Next, ask the child to wiggle fingers independently, without the hands pressed together. Ask the child to wiggle "number 1," then "number 2," and so on.

- Mix them up, asking the child to wiggle 1, then 4, then 3.
- Ask the child to wiggle finger number 1 on the right hand.
- Ask the child to wiggle finger number 3 on the left hand.
- Proceed with the game through successive variations in successive lessons.
- At the first hint of confusion, ask the child to place palms back together to review the order.
- Teach the child the rhyme, sung to the first five tones of the major scale, sing up on "1- 2- 3- 4- 5"; sing down on "sure as I'm alive!"
- Ask her to touch the tips of the appropriate fingers together as you sing the song.

Tunnel trip/ hand position

- Start the child at the piano bench.
- Curve the child's fingers to form a "highway tunnel."
- Next, let the child select a small toy car from the box you have available.
- Decide with the child where their "trip" is to lead—to Grandma's, to New York City, to Disney World.

- Again forming the hand by placing your hand over the child's (so that he learns kinesthetically the feeling of correct hand position), "drive" the little car through the tunnel.
- Point out, "Your hand must stay curved so that your car will be able to pass through the tunnel." Pass the car through both hands repeatedly.
- Give the car to the child so that he can practice at home with the parents, being sure you let parents know how the tunnel game is played.

Finger tappers

- To teach numbering in terms of piano touch, first ask the child to press his hands together with fingertips touching.
- Ask him to tap his fingers together: "Tap the Twos," "Tap the Threes," and so on.
- Now ask him to place his hands on a tabletop.
- Ask him to tap Number Three, Number One, Number Four.
- Give the child a chance to be the teacher and call out the numbers for you to tap.
- Add the concept of right and left, asking him to tap Number Three with the left hand.
- Next, do the same with the right hand, and so on.

Arm staccato

Children learn staccato first by hearing it. Play "Baby Bunnies" (see appendix 3) to demonstrate the staccato sound.

- Explain that staccato means removing your hand quickly.
- Ask the child to practice lifting his hands quickly as you play "Baby Bunnies."
- When you move him to the keyboard, point out that when the bunnies are hopping, you lift your hand away quickly.
- When the bunnies are not hopping, you "pat the bunnies" (this is the beginning of the understanding of legato).
- Let the child try what he's seen and heard.
- "Play" the song on the child's arm.
- Play the first three notes staccato—a tap.
- Play the next notes legato—a touch.
- Ask the child to feel the difference.

I suggest that when you play staccato, you touch the keys as if you were touching a "hot potato." Quickly, and off! Though this exercises mainly whole-arm staccato, it is the first staccato children learn and the one they most often use.

"Hot Cross Buns" (see p. 95) could be presented in the same manner at another lesson.

Wide wings/ arm position

To teach arm position begin with the child standing at the piano. When children are very small, standing helps them best negotiate the whole keyboard.

When the child is seated, place his arms and hands in the best position by guiding him, then show him that as he moves his arms out toward the end of the keyboard, he must move forward. This position permits him to extend much farther.

Use your hands to press gently on the child's shoulders, to show that he can relax his shoulders while moving his arms in a half-circle from his elbows. Gently move the shoulders down, because children sometimes have a tendency to tense up their shoulders in order to keep their elbows at the correct level.

Technique tunes

A series of songs and exercises in appendix 3, including "Bob-White," "Up the Street," "Whip-poor-will," and others, are intended to teach a successively more complex series of technical accomplishments, from arm staccato and legato to hand-over-hand legato, finger legato, arm legato, and staccato in combination, fingering, playing with hands together for the first time, combined with successive challenges in phrasing, sight reading, dynamics, and varying rhythm and tempo.

Complete instructions and goals for using these songs are included in appendix 3.

It's dynamic

The child learns the concept of dynamics by hearing it in action.

- Draw the "hairpin" sign that signifies crescendo or decrescendo, or introduce it from a flash card.
- Play for the child, starting very softly and growing

louder, while explaining to him what you are doing in a voice that begins very softly and grows louder. Since the ability to make songs on the piano is very beguiling to the young child, the concept of dynamics usually is easily absorbed.

- Write the signs for dynamics gradations from *pp* through *ff* on 3" × 5" note cards and place them in order.
- Scramble the cards and make a game of asking the children to put the cards in the correct order. Explain that contrast is important in music and that these signs are meant to make the music louder or softer "than what came before."

Tempi time   Children immediately begin learning tempo variation when they hear songs played fast and slow. Introduce the signs very slowly.

- Begin using the terms for tempo early, always pointing out that these words are "music language" for fast, slow, very fast, and very slow.
- When the child is old enough to be able to read words, show her the words allegro, vivace allegro, largo, and so on.
- Encourage her to play her own compositions in different tempi so that she begins to understand that the words indicate a speed of sound that she can identify.

Fundamentals of performance

Piano parties are some of the happiest, most gratifying times you will have in the studio. Schedule them at least four times a year, because the traditional "once a year" recital places too much pressure on the young child to get "everything right" for the one big day. Several recitals throughout the year also provide more exposure for performing before those important people the child loves and respects. Families are invited to piano parties, as are "guest artists," graduated students who come back to play. They're a marvelous inspiration for the beginners.

I schedule the first piano party near Halloween, soon after the end of the school day to accommodate those children

who are in all-day elementary school. Children can come in costume. The costume need not be full dress—it may simply be a mask—but this gives the child who might still be a bit shy about performing a wonderful opportunity to make music disguised as someone else. We've had some wonderful witches, a monster whose long fingernails provided a challenge, and a cat whose tail had to be kept out of the way.

The second piano party is scheduled to fall just before the winter holiday break, and the third party takes place around Valentine's Day. Sometimes I add a spring party—usually when the children can't wait for another one—but there is always a party just before lessons end for the summer. Provide a printed program for this final party. I try to schedule all parties to fall on the same day of the week.

Children should have the opportunity to choose what songs they will play for the parties—their own compositions or music you help them select. They should be well rehearsed and prepared for the music they will play, because they need the security of knowing exactly what they will do when they approach the keyboard. While the youngest students play, stand beside the piano so that they can see you and you can offer words of encouragement and support, if they need this, while they play.

Teach children to take a bow after they finish to thank the audience for their appreciation of the music they've played for them (this is, after all, a performing art!). Also encourage them to smile, pointing out that smiling is one way they can share the joy of what they are doing. Before parties, take time in class to discuss how to show that they care about their fellow students by sitting quietly while others play during piano parties. Enlist the support and cooperation of parents on this matter. They can discreetly remove a child who isn't able to pay attention to the performance.

Tape each child's name on the chair he will occupy during the party (except, of course, during his own performance), and arrange the chairs so that the children most able to sit quietly next to each other are seated side by side. It is critically important to limit the length of parties to 30 or 40 minutes; young children can't sit still and attend to music—or anything!—for much longer than this, and you want these to be happy, successful occasions.

Parents often provide refreshments for piano parties, and if they are not able to, the teacher provides a treat. Piano parties make the idea of performance meaningful for children. It is my experience that immediately after a party, students come into class eager to begin planning for the next party.

I try to find time, at the end of every party, to speak to each child individually and congratulate him on his performance. It's a special moment of greeting that reinforces the fine work he's done and the pride he justifiably feels. Often, I videotape piano parties and make copies available to the parents. They can provide their own blank tape or reimburse you for this extra expense. This way they can have a record of their children's first efforts as performing artists.

CHAPTER 11

The First Lesson

From small beginnings come great things.
—Proverb

Just as there is no such thing as a "typical" student, there is no such thing as a "typical" lesson. However, as a brief illustration of the way lessons progress in terms of the time given each activity, I am including two lesson plans—one for an early individual lesson and one for a group. Your own early lesson plans may be quite different, and there is no single correct way to proceed. These are only examples.

Bear in mind that group lessons ordinarily do not begin the first week. It is important to match children in groups of two, three or four. More than four gets unmanageable (see chapter 12). Match them by using the information you receive from spending time with them individually. Additionally, young children need time to get to know the teacher and feel comfortable with the idea of musical performance. They are often ready after a few weeks for the second lesson in the week to be held in a group. Group lessons reinforce and build on the skills learned in individual lessons.

It's a good practice to come into every lesson "loaded"; have more material ready than you believe you will ever use, at least until you establish the pace of the individual child. It is far better to leave children wanting more, with activities remaining, than to come up short. Each of these activities lasts no more than two to three minutes, so there will be a surprising amount of variation in 30 minutes. As I have mentioned before, the earliest lessons may not last the full half hour; there are times for getting acquainted and, at first, even a 10-minute lesson may be enough for a child.

I have made a practice of starting lessons in the middle of September to allow children time to first become accustomed to the new environments of preschool or early elementary school. Too many new stimuli all at once can overwhelm a young child.

Ask help from parents in scheduling lessons at a calm, free time of day when the child is rested and not hurrying to get to school or home for a special event. This way, you allow the child to focus more readily on music. Morning can be a very good time for scheduling lessons for the young child, and it allows you the possibility of using your day more efficiently.

The assignment book

The assignment book has a fourfold purpose. It is a device for communicating with the parents about what has been accomplished in a given lesson and what is ahead for the next lesson; it informs the child what to work on at home; it is a tool for praising children on their work and establishing a clear record of their progress; and it becomes the place in which children write the music they have composed and bring to class to be shared.

At the first lesson, give each child one of the wide-spaced music manuscript books with that child's name inscribed, printed, or formed in stick-on letters on the front. Some children like to write their names on the cover of this book. Each assignment that you write in the book should be dated, and each assignment should be in a different color (marker or pen) from the preceding one. These books should be large enough to hold one entire year of assignments, comments, and notes.

Early assignments for the very young child really are assignment messages meant for the parents. It is important to keep parents informed about what you have been working on during the lessons—finding the two black friends, for example. This gives them the opportunity to emphasize those things with the child at home. You may write out the song in numbered, outline form (see "Hot Cross Buns" figure below) as well as noting for the parents what you hope to accomplish at the next lesson.

Later, as the child begins to use music books, you can write in the assignment book the pages to be covered each week and which songs are to be played at home.

You can also note in the assignment book other relevant information, such as which songs the child is working on playing by rote and which theory workbook pages to work on for the next class (see Bibliography for workbook possibilities). Forthcoming parties can also be announced in the assignment book.

As lessons progress, use the assigment book to praise the child—when he or she is very young, by using colored stickers with musical or cartoon themes, later, by writing your own comments on the work accomplished at home: "Excellent!" "Well done!" In my class, six "Excellents!" earn a miniature plastic bust of a composer as a reward.

At those times when work doesn't get done, the best policy is to ignore it. When the child asks why he didn't get a sticker, you might point out, "The assignment needs more work," thus deflecting the correction from the child to the work itself. I make a practice of writing in the assignment book only during the lessons when I am with the child one-on-one, not on group days (it gets too hectic).

The first lesson (individual)

Participants: Teacher and Benjamin, age four. This is Benjamin's first experience with music lessons.

10 a.m. Benjamin arrives with his father, who will stay in the waiting area while Benjamin has his lesson. The teacher greets Benjamin with the sincere courtesy that is so effective with young children: "Welcome to piano lessons. It's wonderful to see you. Do your parents call you Benjamin or Ben? Good, Ben, let's put on our music shoes." Ben hangs up his jacket on the coat rack placed specially at the children's height and slips off his street shoes and puts on the soft cloth slippers that will be kept in a basket by the door of the studio, clipped together by a clothespin with his name on it.

10:05 a.m. Ben and the teacher enter the studio. If the child is a bit reluctant to leave his or her parent behind, it's perfectly acceptable to invite the parent into the studio during the lesson. (It won't take long for Ben to become comfortable leaving his parent in the waiting area.) The teacher and Ben explore the studio. The teacher points out Ben's special chair; it has his name on it, and the teacher makes that clear, even if Ben isn't reading yet. He will want to inspect the musical toys, the pictures, and the supplies in the studio, and these activities will help him feel comfortable.

10:08 a.m. The teacher tells Ben, "We're going to take a picture of you at the piano. We'll put it up with all the other students' pictures right here." Ben sits down at the piano and the teacher takes an instant picture. They watch the picture develop, show it to Ben's father, and then ceremoniously mount it on the wall. Now it's time to share: "Ben, what is the name of your school? Who is your special friend there? What is your favorite ice cream flavor? Do you have a favorite song? Can you sing it with me?" (Favorite nursery school songs often can form the basis for later lessons in tempo, dynamics, and rhythm.)

10:12 a.m. The teacher plays "Hello, Ev'rybody" (see appendix 1) for Ben, using his name. (In later lessons, the hello song will be used as the basis for demonstrating many musical concepts.)

10:13 a.m. The teacher brings Ben to sit beside him or her at the keyboard. "Can you hold up two fingers?" The teacher and Ben hold up two fingers. "Now, how about three fingers?" Returning Ben to two fingers, the teacher says: "These two fingers are friends. They're side by side.

Let's look at the keyboard. Can you find the two black friends, side by side?" The teacher and Ben work together to find the two and three black friends. Then, putting the child's hand over hers, the teacher plays the two black and three black friends, going up the piano. "Let's go *up* the piano and find them. Now, let's go *down* the piano and find them."

10:15 a.m. "Ben," the teacher asks, "can you be a little bird and find a listening corner?" Once Ben is settled, the teacher plays "Hot Cross Buns" on the two and three black keys (see p. 95).

10:17 a.m. Back at the piano, the teacher demonstrates, then leads Ben to play the first three descending notes of "Hot Cross Buns" (it's very important that he leave the first day able to play something). With the teacher, then possibly on his own, Ben plays B, A, G. The teacher might invite Ben to stand at the keyboard. Some, especially those with older brothers or sisters who play piano, may want to sit on a stool that can be raised or lowered).

10:20 a.m. The teacher plays "Hello Ev'rybody," only now with a "goodbye" emphasis (see appendix 1) for Ben, then offers him a choice of treats. "You've done a wonderful job. I'll see you again soon."

10:22 a.m. While Ben is changing slippers and getting his coat, the teacher writes the date in his assignment book, and "Welcome to Music Lessons!" Next, she writes Ben's assignment to do at home:

1. Find the two black friends.
2. Find the three black friends.
3. Find them all over the piano.

The teacher gives Ben's father Ben's workbook and writes down the two or three pages (no more) that Ben and his parents can do together at home. She uses a different colored marker for each week's assignment, so parents can readily see the progression at a glance.

Matching students for group lessons

It is very important to match students in groups of two, three, or four only after you have had at least one, probably two, and possibly several individual lessons to observe their behavior.

Many factors come into play in matching students, some of which are not always immediately apparent. For example, at the ages of four or five, some boys are at a developmental stage in which they find it difficult to be surrounded by girls, though they may play happily one on one with an individual girl. This is a process of building identity and no cause for alarm, but it often is easier to match a boy of this age with another boy, so that the message comes through loud and clear that other boys really enjoy piano lessons just as he does.

General factors to look for in the matching process include the following:

• GENDER: It's sometimes best to try to match children of the same sex, especially with boys. But this is definitely not a hard-and-fast rule. I have had very good luck matching high-energy girls with quieter boys, with the students relating well and developing an appreciation for one another. In a time where parents seem particularly eager to help remove traditional boy-girl distinctions, such matches can work very well.

• AGE AND SCHOOL: Matching an older four and a younger four, both of whom are in nursery school, may be a better idea than matching an older four with a five-year-old who has already begun kindergarten. School experience is much on the minds of young children, and they need a sense of being with their peers. Grade levels of more than one year become even more significant when the children reach elementary-school age.

• PERSONALITY: Is a child active or complacent, shy or outgoing? How does the child seem to relate to other children? Rely on your instinct to match groups that will have a dynamic experience together, and this may not always mean pairing those children who are very shy or those who are very outgoing. Matching a contemplative but eager student with a more physically active child may help one to temper his responses and the other to come forward a bit more. Similarly, you could pair a natural leader with a follower, but then work to give the follower leadership opportunities, to the benefit of both children.

- LEARNING STYLE: Observe carefully the ways children respond. Does one grasp new concepts quickly and then work methodically on the finishing touches? Is another child quick to absorb as many experiences as possible, without paying a great deal of attention to any specific one? All of these will be factors in combining groups, so that no child is overwhelmed and no child is bored.

- PARENTS' SCHEDULES: This may be the least critical factor, but it is one for you to consider wherever possible. Children who seem to "go together" well and whose parents have compatible schedules should be placed together if possible.

Matching can be an intimidating process, because it is so important for the children's success and greatly affects their attitude and degree of eagerness toward lessons. Bear in mind that no group is set in stone. Give a match a few months to settle, but if there are problems, feel confident in rearranging things. Semester breaks may be natural times to reconstitute groupings. Remember also that the process of matching grows easier and more instinctive as your experience with young children grows.

Sample group lesson

Participants: The teacher; Ben, four; Sarah, four; and Daniel, five. Ben, Sarah, and Daniel have been matched according to information about their abilities and personalities that the teacher has garnered during the early weeks of individual lessons. Daniel, because he is just a little older, may be the natural leader, but these roles will shift and realign as time passes.

10 a.m. The children arrive, are greeted, quickly hang up their coats, and slip on their music shoes. (They're veterans now, and know the routine.)

10:02 a.m. The children sit down in their chairs in the studio for the hello song. The teacher then asks, "Shall I play it high now? Shall I play it low?" (Every effort is made, consistently, to give children a choice.) The teacher progresses through playing the song loudly and softly.

10:04 a.m. The children get up to go to the piano and find the two and three black keys. While one child is playing, the other two have the role of "directing." "Shall Ben play the two black friends high or low?"

10:06 a.m. The teacher sets out the cards that will teach the rudiments of left and right (see p. 84). He has drawn mittens with the thumbs pointing left or right on each of the cards. At first, the cards are in primary colors (all the right hands, for example, are red and all the left hands are blue). Later, they're in black on white cards and the children must rely on finding the direction of the thumbs. The teacher distributes the cards and each child is asked to take his or her cards with the thumb pointing left on top and stack them on top of the card on the piano bench that has the thumb pointing left. Next, each child repeats the process with the cards that have the thumb pointing right.

10:09 a.m. The teacher suggests, "Let's be listening birds. What kind of bird are you? What color are you?" She then asks them each to find a listening corner. The teacher plays "Hot Cross Buns," which by now many of the children have learned to play.

10:11 a.m. The children come to the piano to first clap out, then play "Hot Cross Buns." (The repetition strengthens the mastery of this now-familiar piece and the "directors" demonstrate their knowledge of keyboard geography by asking their counterparts to play "high" or "low.")

10:15 a.m. The teacher asks the children to sit down on the floor and sits down with them. It's time for the first of the movement games, the activities that build coordination and musical concepts (see appendix 2). The first one is "See-Saw." The children move their extended arms up and down to the music, first pointing out what color seesaw each has chosen to be.

10:20 a.m. "Let's each pick up an imaginary ball," suggests the teacher. "What color is your ball, Sarah? Ben, is yours red?" The children "bounce" and "toss" the imaginary balls to music.

10:22 a.m. The teacher passes out the soft plastic balls and gives the children a few moments to get used to the feel of them. Then they pass the balls to "Hot Cross Buns," slowly at first. They can also roll or toss the balls as they grow accustomed to using them.

10:26 a.m. It's time for the good-bye song. The teacher bids Sarah, Ben, and Daniel good-bye.

Lesson length

A piano teacher sells expertise rather than time, so it's important for parents to understand why, even though an "average" lesson may last for half an hour, some early lessons may end after 10 or 20 minutes. Later lessons may be scheduled for 40 minutes, but only for older children (these are specially scheduled). Discussing this with parents earlier, pointing out that children need to leave a lesson wanting more—long before the first signs of boredom appear—will help enlist their agreement and understanding. Parents will readily offer support once they see that the teacher's decision about time in the studio is based on building the child's lifelong appreciation of music, and that every minute is an important stroke on that canvas. Let them know, as well, that the mood of an individual child and the composition of a particular group also are important factors when determining the length of a lesson.

Parents can help here by informing the teacher of any changes or potential distractions in a child's schedule that can have an impact on the lesson. In the same way, parents with busy schedules may need to understand why it is sometimes a good idea to continue to work on a project or skill even if the work runs over the ordinary allotted time. As the years of lessons progress, and the age and capability of children grow, the lesson often will be *scheduled* to last more than half an hour, though not more than 40 minutes. In general, scheduling lessons for 30 minutes, allowing 10 minutes of "selvage," means scheduling 40 minutes per child.

CHAPTER 12

Putting It All Together

Music creates order out of chaos, for rhythm imposes unanimity upon the divergent, melody imposes continuity upon the disjointed, and harmony imposes compatibility upon the incongruous.
—*Yehudi Menuhin*

The final chapter of a book like this traditionally is the place, as I once heard an author say, where you deposit "everything that didn't fit anywhere else." In this last chapter, I discuss, fittingly enough, endings, that is, the process of graduating the young child to private lessons with a different instructor. But I also will cover potential difficulties and business arrangements—all of which are critical topics in the work of teaching piano to the young child.

The difficult child or reluctant learner

Most difficulties with children in piano class are minor and transitory. They can be the result of illness, guests at home, new experiences at school, or a host of other changes. Directing behavior positively in class, changing activities more frequently for children who seem unable to stick to something, and altering the pace of the lesson usually will take care of most problems.

In those rare instances when problems continue, the first defense is enlisting the help of the parents. Give the parent the opportunity to explain what might be troubling the child—is a parent away on a business trip, for example? Is a new baby creating some anxieties? Insistence on "practicing" at home may interfere with success at the lesson for some children; they may feel that they are not meeting their parents' expectations. This can taint the whole atmosphere of lessons, but it's readily corrected by working with the parents to ease off and understand how very well their child actually is adapting and learning this new skill.

Children who seem to be using fractious or attention-getting negative behavior may be reacting to a situation at home that parents aren't even aware is a problem. It is likely at some point you will be teaching a child whose parents are separating or going through a divorce. This is an enormously unsettling and distracting experience for any child, and it has an impact on all aspects of his or her life. Few piano teachers are also qualified crisis counselors or therapists. Still, you will probably be one of the most significant adult figures in a child's life (after all, most children don't even see their grandparents twice each week). In that role, you can help simply by seriously listening. You also can be sensitive to their emotions within the context of the music lessons.

Occasionally, a child will come along whose behavior cannot be adjusted sufficiently to allow lessons to continue. Perhaps it's a question of maturity—a few months down the line, all may be well. But in those cases where a child's persistent inability to participate in the lesson threatens the equilibrium of the rest of the group or the process of learning piano, you should feel confident about removing that child from a lesson (for a day, with the parents' cooperation, or even permanently). Repeated disruptive or negative behavior that persists over a period of time is a clear signal you should begin evaluating whether that student should continue lessons.

It is always worth remembering that young children at this stage of development differ greatly in ability. This means that children may be surging ahead in some areas while catching up in others. Many four- and five-year-old children can write and read, for example, but just as many others, from equally supportive and child-centered homes, cannot. Other reasons for the seeming inability to learn may be emotional, since young children don't always express their problems verbally.

Finally, your own presentation of material on a given day may not be appropriate for a given child. The beauty of lessons is that, in just a day or two, you'll have another chance to present the material in another way.

Graduating students

Like parents, you will feel enormous pride and some nostalgia when your young students "outgrow" the work they have done with you. Some of the same emotions that pertain to a first grade teacher saying farewell to students who learned to read with his love and support are involved with graduating young piano students when they reach the age of seven (sometimes, if I feel a child is not ready to move on, I will continue teaching her until she is eight or nine). Yet, like parents, you will also realize that continued growth means new stimulus and new environments.

There are several reasons—some practical, some subtle—why graduating is essential. First, moving children along to another capable teacher when the time is right frees you to concentrate on the incoming crop of very young students. Once you undertake this work, with all the commitment and preparation it requires, you will want to give as many children as possible the benefit of this teaching. That would be impossible if you continued to teach every child with whom you began lessons.

Some teachers continue to teach a few of their older students as private pupils. Depending on the nature of the child and the relationships, this can work. In general, however, it is possible for the children and their first piano teacher to become almost "too comfortable" together, thereby inhibiting continued artistic growth, which can be stimulated by new challenges.

The limits are flexible, of course, but generally a child who begins lessons at age three or four will be ready to move on by age seven. My students tend to see me with great affection but as their "baby" piano teacher. When you present graduation to them as proof of their mastery and their readiness to study piano in even more depth, they usually take pride in the event, seeing it as part of the important process of growing up.

Begin the process of graduation with the parents, by informing them (many months in advance, if possible) that the time is approaching. Work with parents to select a suitable new teacher, drawing on your own network in the community, or serving as a resource where parents can check their own choices. This is a potentially stressful time of change for parents, too, who have grown to trust and rely on their child's first piano teacher.

Help the parents understand how important it is that the child not be informed of the upcoming change until almost the last day of lessons. The information can be upsetting, since (we hope) the bond between a young child and a teacher is a strong one. When the time comes, explain that this is a happy time and means that the child is ready for a new experience. Emphasize the "growing up" aspects of the change, likening it to moving from first grade to second grade and changing teachers. Assure the child that he or she will be welcome and invited back as a guest artist at piano parties and for visits.

At this time, it's important for the child (and everyone) to know exactly who the new teacher will be. Your approval of that new teacher will be important to the child as well. As a final gift, I have often presented a bust of a composer to mark what is, indeed, a very significant occasion. Other teachers have provided certificates with the child's name that can be placed on the child's wall. This is the time to give the family the audio- and videotapes of the child's long history in piano class to save as treasured keepsakes.

If you remain in your community for several years or more, it will not be difficult to follow your students through the years of their future study, especially since you may be teaching their younger siblings. You will find that their early base in piano has meant that they are better students at whatever instrument they may consider studying.

The business of teaching piano

At the beginning of this book, I pointed out that it is my belief that instructors of piano for the young child are teaching people first, curriculum second. Yet, ideally, the teacher of piano for the young child should be the most accomplished, most talented of performers, whose love of the instrument is passionate.

The economic reality for all artists, however, whether they are actors, dancers, writers, visual artists, or musicians, is a hard one. Unless they derive a significant portion of income from teaching at an institution (public school, university, or conservatory) making a living at private lessons is difficult. It is difficult even when there is another reliable income in the household, and for a young teacher, whose reputation in a community is not yet well established, it can be hard indeed.

You probably teach because you are called to teach. It is possible to make a living, because teaching piano to the very young child lets you make important use of the morning hours. But before you set up or rent a studio, take an inventory of your circumstances, asking yourself such questions as these:

- Have I considered the reality that my teaching may not afford me such basics as sick leave, medical insurance, or a retirement policy?
- Are my basic needs, such as housing, assured?
- Do I have sufficient resources to equip or rent a studio given the income I will derive from teaching? Compute this income based on the minimum number of students you expect to teach.
- Do I have a sufficient network of potential students and referrals from other teachers to attract the business I need?
- Are my family needs and responsibilities such that I can devote the time this work requires?

Once you have a satisfactory answer to all these questions, make an inventory of all those expenses that will be tax deductible. Many artists have a notorious avoidance complex when it comes to the financial implications of their work, but these considerations can make an enormous difference.

Potentially tax-deductible expenses can be:

- THE STUDIO: its cost, if it is an addition to your home; its rent outside the home; a percentage of the interest portion of the mortgage and depreciation, along with a portion of each year's total utility bills if the studio is set up in an existing home.

• INSTRUMENTS AND EQUIPMENT: the piano and rhythm instruments; audio and video equipment; a computer used in studio business; records, tapes, books, tables, chairs, and waiting-room furnishings. Depending on the nature of the equipment and some tax considerations, you can often deduct either the purchase price of the equipment as a one-time expense, or depreciate (deduct portions of it) over a number of years.

• SUPPLIES: office supplies such as business cards, stationery, and pens, including items that might be needed for mailings.

• PROFESSIONAL DEVELOPMENT OPPORTUNITIES: classes, workshops, conventions, membership dues, subscriptions, and books.

• MISCELLANY: auto expense, advertising, recital expenses, accountant's fees, phone calls for a direct teaching purpose (e.g., organizing recitals), and piano tuning.

A strict accounting, on a personal computer or in a ledger, can help make a yearly total of all these deductions readily accessible.

I cannot overemphasize the importance of consulting a professional tax advisor. The above is presented only to help get you started thinking about managing the taxes related to your business, not to provide professional advice. Like you, I intend to stick with what I know: teaching. Keep in mind that keeping receipts is just as important as keeping records, and that the tax law changes frequently. Seeking a specialist's help might cost a few dollars, but could save much money and grief in the long run.

Building a practice

Most of your students will come to you by word of mouth, as the important things you are doing with young children and the piano spreads through your community. But in the early days, you can take advantage of many community resources to help spread your message. An aggressive marketing campaign often makes artists uncomfortable, but the service you are providing is an important one, and people will welcome opportunities to learn more about it.

Making yourself available as a "guest artist" for a program of a day or several days at local kindergartens and preschools often is a welcome experience for children and a rich source of new students. When you perform, display brochures that describe the kind of work you do with the young child along with your music program. Relationships with symphony members and orchestra conductors in your community can be a source of referrals, as can connections with church musicians. Some musicians have had good results distributing brochures to be included with the local Welcome Wagon materials for new families. Other teachers target a neighborhood and place their brochures door-to-door—an effective and inexpensive marketing tool.

A professional-looking and comprehensive brochure can be put together by a local graphic designer—a one-time expense. Don't include your fees, as these can change from year to year and make your "new" brochures suddenly obsolete. Your brochure can provide a basic description of the program you offer, and can serve as an effective introduction when you perform, teach, lecture, and travel. Brochures can be displayed at local music stores, preschools, libraries, universities, and conservatories, even markets.

Take advantage of the free opportunity for "advertising" offered by local newspapers and radio stations, which often will include an announcement of your performances or your lessons in community calendar sections. Perhaps most effective of all are the "networking" and sharing between you and other music professionals, including other teachers and tuners.

Accepting students and the waiting list

Before you know it, you will have a waiting list of children whose parents hope they will be able to enter your next year's classes. Though you will want to honor the waiting list as much as possible, do so with an eye to keeping control of the composition of your classes, as this is the critical factor. For example, if you are getting too many boys, too many girls, or too many older students, you may have to drop down on the list to achieve greater diversity. Parents' schedules are important, too. You may have openings that can accommodate children whose names are lower down on your waiting list.

Keep a log of the names, addresses, and phone numbers of parents who contact you during the year. At the time of the initial inquiry, give them a date when they can call back to check on the availability of classes. It is then best to rely on the parents to make the second contact. The parents who take the initiative to call back often will make the most enthusiastic and committed piano parents.

In certain cases, it may be appropriate to contact families when an unforeseen vacancy has occurred, but it can be distracting for the piano teacher to follow up when families may have moved, changed their minds, or found other teachers.

Upcoming classes should be formed no later than midsummer, though inevitable changes will occur during the weeks when classes begin.

Determining fees

The preschool piano teacher should be the most highly paid piano instructor in the neighborhood. It may sound like an impossible ideal, but consider the range of abilities and skills you must employ to do this important work. You combine a comprehensive and authoritative knowledge of your discipline with your skill in child development and teaching techniques for the young child. In the first years, a wider range of skills is demanded of the teacher; as the child grows in capability, that range narrows.

Gather information from local music professionals' organizations in setting up your fee schedule, using your community's cost-of-living numbers as part of your analysis. For example, lessons on the Upper West Side of Manhattan will be priced differently from those in a small town in Nebraska—but then, your cost of living needs will differ in those two areas as well.

Set forth your fees in the initial parent interview, and at that time set up a payment schedule, on a full-year, semester, or monthly basis. If a verbal exchange about costs feels difficult, prepare a fee schedule with a place for a parent's signature. This document also can set forth other studio policies about such matters as cancelled lessons, piano parties, and practice at home. In addition, this document sometimes is useful, since it can be discussed at home if both parents can't attend the orientation meeting.

A brief coda

We have reached the end of one story and the beginning of another. The story you will write as an accomplished teacher of piano to the young child is already in process or is just beginning. It will be a story of hope and excitement, hard work and joy, in which you are strengthened as a musician, and tested as an artist and as a human being. In the end, you will have touched the lives of young children as few adults can. When they pass from your studio, it will be through the door you have opened, into a larger world of artistic richness. As your students grow and progress and touch the lives of others, they will be continuing proof of the powerful legacy of the art habit. As the old rhyme says, they will have music wherever they go.

That music will make their homes, their community, wherever they live, better places. Perhaps the music your children play, and the effect you and the music have had on their lives will do its own small, graceful part to lead in time to a better world.

"Hello, Ev'rybody"

**by Eunice Holsaert
and Charity Bailey**

Music Games

Purpose The purposes of these music games are to develop ease at the keyboard, and facility and precision in playing for the preschool and early elementary grades. In addition, the games provide interest, variety, movement, and rhythmic action for the young child during the lesson.

Presentation The presentation is done away from the piano, standing or sitting on the floor or a chair, singing the songs (with piano accompaniment) while performing the actions with rhythmic precision.

1. See-Saw
2. Humpty-Dumpty
3. Bow-Wow-Wow
4. Baa, Baa, Black Sheep
5. Deedle, Deedle, Dumpling
6. Bobby Shafto I
7. Pussy Cat
8. Little Tommy Titmouse
9. Large Shears
10. Jack and Jill
11. The King of France
12. Wheels
13. Rockie Row
14. Two Little Blackbirds
15. Bobby Shafto II

16. Pease Porridge Hot
17. The Man in the Moon
18. Little Boy Blue
19. One, Two, Three
20. Medium Shears
21. Mistress Mary
22. Small Shears
23. Trot, Trot, Trot
24. Little Tommy Tucker
25. Little Jumping Joan
26. Drums
27. Little Miss Muffet
28. Jack Be Nimble
29. Willy, Willy Wilkin
30. London Bridge Is Falling Down
31. Baby Shears
32. Farmer in the Dell
33. Ride a Cock-Horse
34. Mulberry Bush
35. Tick Tock

See-Saw

Purpose   Control and freedom of motion from the shoulder.

Position   Standing, with arms at shoulder level, held out straight to the side—hands extended with palms down—fingers together, straight, with thumbs outstretched.

Action   On the first of each measure, one arm raises straight up to the side of the head as the other arm lowers to the side of the body. Repeat on the first beat of each measure.

1. SEE-SAW

Slowly

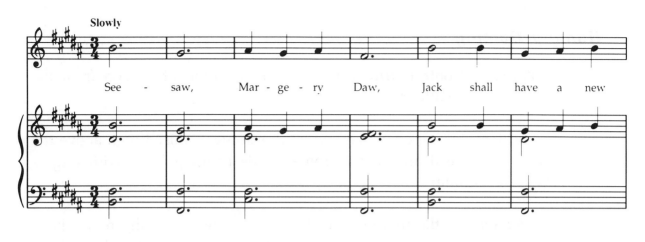

See - saw, Mar - ge - ry Daw, Jack shall have a new

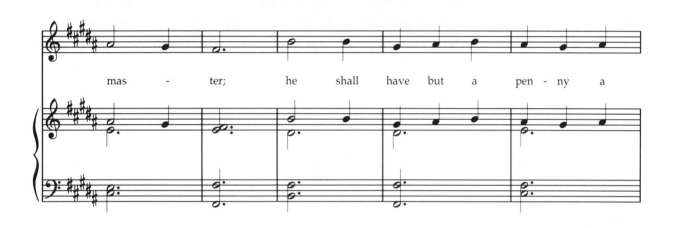

mas - ter; he shall have but a pen - ny a

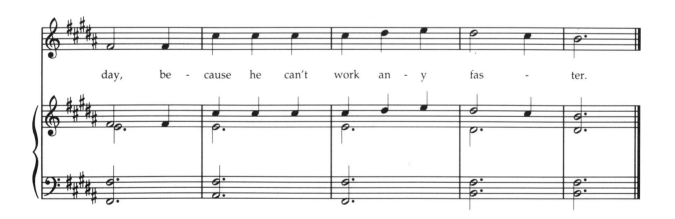

day, be - cause he can't work an - y fas - ter.

Humpty-Dumpty

Purpose   Control, arm relaxation, and freedom of motion from the shoulder.

Position   Sitting on a chair, with arms straight, raised high above the head and to the front—hands hanging loose with fingers limp.

Action   At the first beats of the music, begin swaying hands back and forth. On the word "fall," let arms drop limply to sides. Hands and fingers stay limp on the floor until music ends. (Teacher may ask, "Is Humpty-Dumpty really broken?" in order to admire the total relaxation of the children's arms.)

2. HUMPTY-DUMPTY

Bow-Wow-Wow

Purpose Individualization of third fingers and control of fingers from third joint (joint closest to palm).

Position Sitting on a chair or the floor, forearms raised to front— hands extended, palms up, fingers straightened, thumbs outstretched.

Action On the first beat of each measure, third fingers raise toward palm, then return to straight out.

3. BOW-WOW-WOW

Bow - wow - wow! Whose dog art thou?

Lit - tle Tom - my Tin - ker's dog, bow - wow - wow!

Baa, Baa, Black Sheep

Purpose	Individualization of thumbs and control from third joints (joints nearest the palm).
Position	Sitting on a chair or the floor, forearms out to front, palms up, fingers straight, thumbs outstretched.
Action	On the first beat of each measure, thumbs cross palms, then go back to straight position on the second beat.

4. BAA, BAA, BLACK SHEEP

Baa, baa, black sheep, have you an - y wool? Yes, Sir, yes, Sir,

three bags full. One for my Mas - ter, one for my

Dame, but none for the naugh - ty boy that cries in the lane.

Deedle, Deedle, Dumpling _____

Purpose	Freedom of motion from shoulders. Coordination.
Position	Standing, with one arm straight up, at the side of the head—one straight down at the side of the body. Hands extended, palms facing the body, fingers straight.
Action	On the first beat of each measure, arms exchange positions, one swinging up, the other swinging down. Elbows should not bend.

Bobby Shafto I _____

Purpose	Control, rotary turn of forearm from elbow.
Position	Standing, with forearms raised out in front of the body. Hands extended, palms down, fingers straight, thumbs outstretched.
Action	On first and third beats of each measure, turn forearms from elbow as far as possible each way in a rotary movement.

5. DEEDLE, DEEDLE, DUMPLING

Dee-dle, dee-dle, dump-ling, my son John! Went to bed with his stock-ings on; one shoe off and one shoe on! Dee-dle, dee-dle, dump-ling, my son John!

6. BOBBY SHAFTO I

Bob - by Shaf - to's gone to sea, sil - ver buck - les on his knee; he'll come back and stay with me, ___ dear Bob - by Shaf - to.

Pussy Cat

Purpose   Individualization of second fingers. Control from third joints (those nearest the palm).

Position   Sitting on a chair or on the floor, forearms out to front, palms up, fingers straight, thumbs outstretched.

Action   On the first beat of each measure, second fingers raise toward palms. On the second beat, they return to straight.

7. PUSSY CAT

Pus - sy cat, pus - sy cat, where have you been? I've been to Lon - don to vis - it the Queen. Pus - sy cat, pus - sy cat, what did _ you there? I fright-ened a lit - tle mouse un - der the chair.

accel.

Little Tommy Titmouse _____

Purpose   Individualization of fifth fingers. Control from third joints.

Position   Sitting, with forearms to front, palms up, fingers straight, thumbs outstretched.

Action   On the first beat of each measure, fifth fingers raise toward palms, then return back to straight position. Teacher may gently waggle child's fifth finger to show how well it moves.

Large Shears _____

Purpose   Freedom and elasticity from shoulders.

Position   Standing, with arms at shoulder level—hands extended, palms to front, fingers together with thumbs outstretched.

Action   On the first beat of each measure, arms cross in front, then return to sides. Keep arms straight throughout, at shoulder level. This exercise will be repeated later for wrist and finger control (middle-sized and small shears).

8. LITTLE TOMMY TITMOUSE

Lit - tle Tom - my Tit - mouse sat up - on a rail. Nid - dle nod - dle went his head, wig - gle wag - gle wag - gle went his __ tail.

accel.

9. LARGE SHEARS

Shear the ___ sheep and trim the ___ tree, but let the lit - tle ___ lamb go free.

Jack and Jill _____

Purpose Control and freedom of motion of arms separately.

Position Seated on a chair, hands flat in front and to the center of lap.

Action At the beginning of the music, arms raise, slowly, high to front, hands and fingers limp. Hold the high position. On the word "Jack," fifth measure, one hand drops to lap—the other drops on "Jill," seventh measure. Hands remain limp on lap until music ends.

10. JACK AND JILL

Jack and Jill went up the hill to fetch a pail of

wa - ter. Jack fell down and broke his crown and

Jill came tumb - ling af - ter.

accel.

The King of France

Purpose   Individualization, independence of third fingers.

Position   Sitting on the floor, with hands in front, palms down and fingers gently folded under.

Action   Third fingers tap on "King." All the other fingers tap on "forty thousand men." On "drew," hands curl up and rock from fingers to wrist. On "put," fingers hide behind back.

Wheels

Purpose   Arm control.

Position   Sides—hands extended, palms facing back.

Action   One arm at a time, very slowly, starts raising to the front, making large arm circles in each measure.

11. THE KING OF FRANCE

The King of France and for-ty thou-sand men drew their swords and put them back a-gain.

12. WHEELS

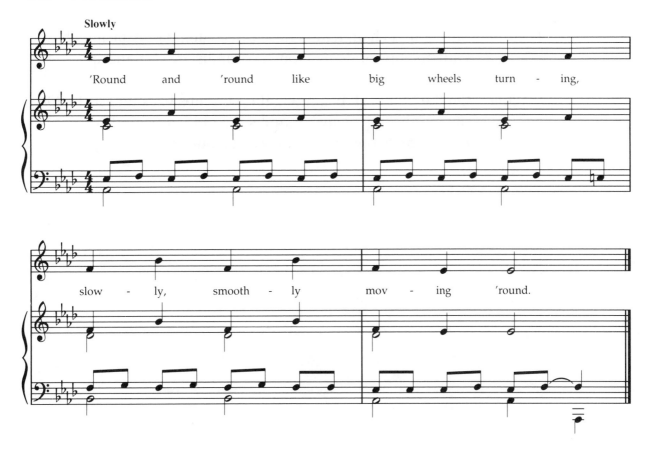

'Round and 'round like big wheels turn - ing, slow - ly, smooth - ly mov - ing 'round.

Rockie Row

Purpose   Elasticity of wrist and coordination.

Position   Sitting on floor with hands straight up on fingertips, palms facing down, thumbs outstretched.

Action   On the first and third beats of measures, one hand slowly rolls forward. The other hand rolls back and flattens on the floor.

Two Little Blackbirds

Purpose   Thumb control from all thumb joints.

Position   Sitting in a chair, hands raised to center, palms facing chest. Only the tips of fingers touch. Thumbs are straight up.

Action   On the first beat, begin wiggling thumbs back and forth. On the words "Fly away," thumbs are hidden behind hand. On the words "Come back," they come out again.

13. ROCKIE ROW

Rock - ie row, rock - ie row, rock - ie, rock - ie, rock we go.

14. TWO LITTLE BLACKBIRDS

There were two black - birds sit - ting on a hill— the one named Jack, the

o - ther named Jill.

Speak: Fly away, Jack, fly away, Jill. Come again, Jack, come again, Jill.

o - ther named Jill.

Bobby Shafto II

Purpose Control. Rotary turn of whole arm from shoulder.

Position Standing, with arms at shoulder level, straight out to front with hands extended. Palms down, fingers together, straight with thumbs outstretched.

Action On the first and third beats of each measure, arms turn as far as possible in each direction in a rotary movement.

15. BOBBY SHAFTO II

Bob - by Shaf - to's gone to sea, sil - ver buck - les on his knee;

he'll come back and stay with me, __ dear Bob - by Shaf - to.

Pease Porridge Hot _____

Purpose Arm independence and coordination.

Position Sitting on floor, with one arm raised high in front, the other resting on the floor, with hand flat.

Action On the first and third beats of each measure, arms exchange position, rhythmically, one going up as the other comes down.

16. PEASE PORRIDGE HOT

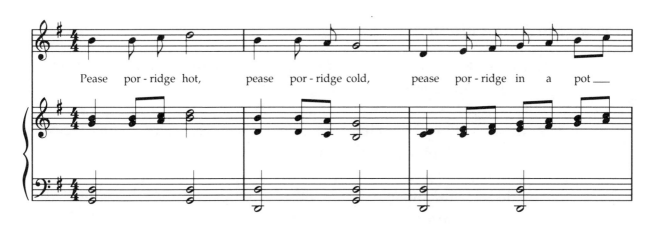

Pease por - ridge hot, pease por - ridge cold, pease por - ridge in a pot ___

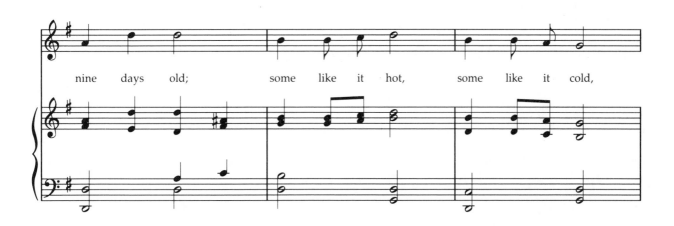

nine days old; some like it hot, some like it cold,

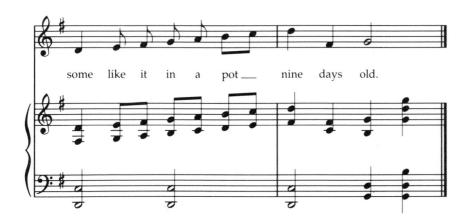

some like it in a pot ___ nine days old.

The Man in the Moon _____

Purpose   Independence of movement. Flexibility of first and second finger joints.

Position   Sitting in a chair, forearms raised vertically, palms facing each other, fingers gently curved with tips touching.

Action   Third fingers start standing straight. On first beats of each measure, thirds fold down and then straighten again from the second joints.

17. THE MAN IN THE MOON

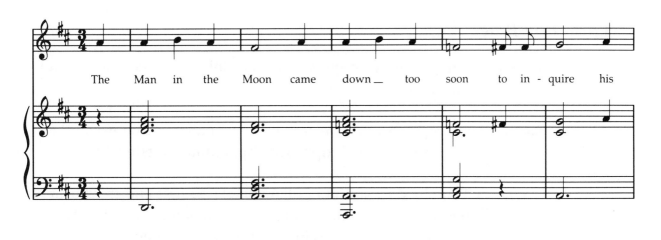

The Man in the Moon came down _ too soon to in-quire his

way to Nor - wich. He went by the south and

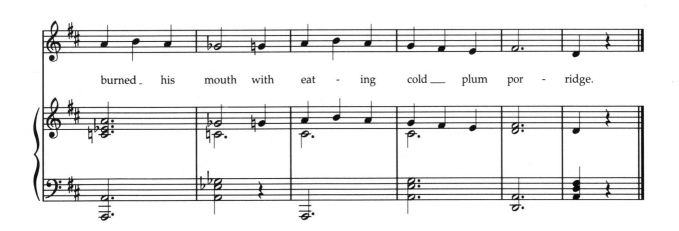

burned _ his mouth with eat - ing cold _ plum por - ridge.

Little Boy Blue

Purpose Independence of movement. Flexibility of first and second finger joints.

Position Sitting with forearms up vertically, palms facing each other, fingers folded with tips touching, thumbs outstretched.

Action Thumbs start straight outstretched. On first and third beats, thumbs fold in and out from nail joints. On the word "Under," tuck thumbs in while speaking the question.

18. LITTLE BOY BLUE

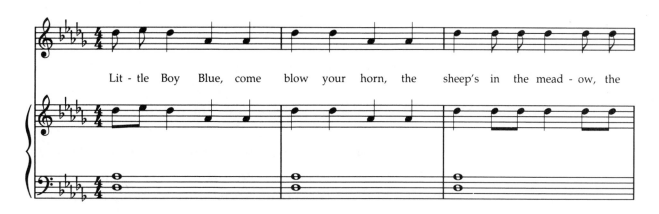

Lit - tle Boy Blue, come blow your horn, the sheep's in the mead - ow, the

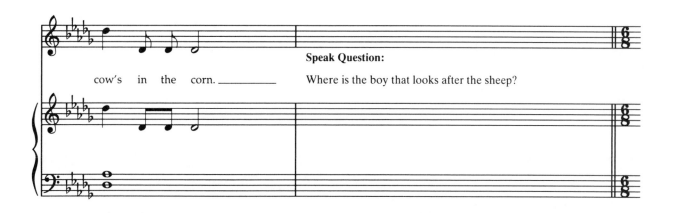

cow's in the corn. _____

Speak Question:

Where is the boy that looks after the sheep?

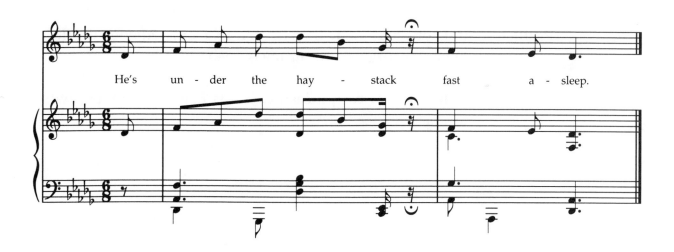

He's un - der the hay - stack fast a - sleep.

One, Two, Three

Purpose   Flexibility. Control from shoulder.

Position   Standing, with arms at sides, and palms to body.

Action   Arms should swing freely from shoulders with elbows straight. On the first beat, arms swing up and clap hands overhead. On the second beat, arms swing down against the sides. Two actions to each measure.

Medium Shears

Purpose   Coordination. Control.

Position   Sitting or standing, with hands straight, crossed one over the other at the wrist, palms facing outward.

Action   On first beat of each measure, hands flap stiffly in and out like a pair of shears.

19. ONE, TWO, THREE

One, two, three, says she to me; one and two make three, you see!

20. MEDIUM SHEARS

Shear the sheep and trim the tree, but let the lit-tle lamb go free.

Mistress Mary ────────────────────────────

Purpose Individualization. Control from third joints.

Position Sitting, with forearms to front. Palms up, fingers straight, thumbs outstretched.

Action On first beat of each measure, fourth fingers raise toward palms, then return to straight position.

21. MISTRESS MARY

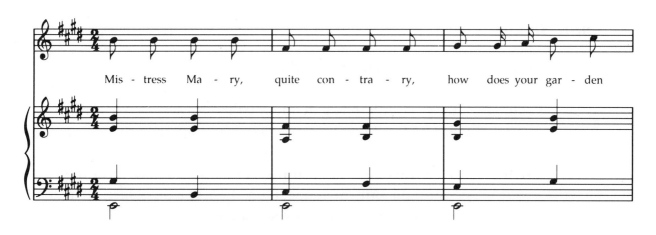

Mis - tress Ma - ry, quite con - tra - ry, how does your gar - den

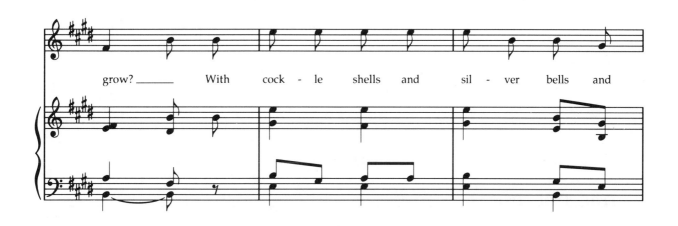

grow? _____ With cock - le shells and sil - ver bells and

pret - ty maids all in a row!

Small Shears

Purpose   Finger independence and control.

Position   Sitting, with hands extended, palms turned downward, second and third fingers straight out like a pair of shears.

Action   On the first beat of each measure, second and third fingers go straight out, then together, then spread apart, then together, like the motion of a scissors.

Trot, Trot, Trot

Purpose   Action of hand from supported wrist.

Position   Sitting on floor, hands centered in front, wrists resting on floor, hands raised straight with fingers curved, thumb out.

Action   On first and third beats of each measure, fingertips drop to floor, then spring back from the wrists in one quick action.

22. SMALL SHEARS

Shear the _____ sheep and trim the _____ tree, but let the lit - tle _____ lamb go free.

23. TROT, TROT, TROT

Trot, trot, trot, po - ny, quick-ly trot. Where 'tis smooth and where 'tis sto - ny, trot a - long, my lit - tle po - ny, trot and nev - er stop! Po - ny, quick-ly trot!

Little Tommy Tucker

Purpose   Independence of fingers, flexibility, first and second joints.

Position   Sitting, with forearms up, palms facing with fingertips touching lightly.

Action   Second fingers begin standing straight. On first and third beats of measures, fold down and back from first and second joints.

24. LITTLE TOMMY TUCKER

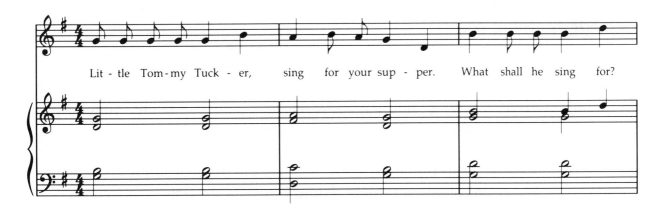

Lit - tle Tom-my Tuck - er, sing for your sup - per. What shall he sing for?

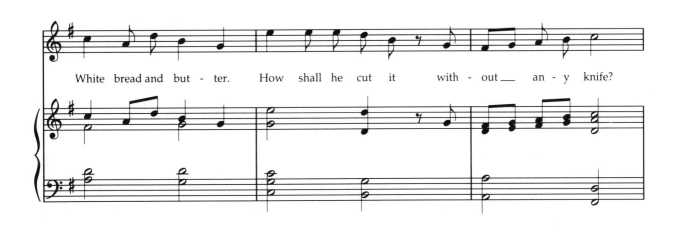

White bread and but - ter. How shall he cut it with - out __ an - y knife?

How shall he mar - ry with - out __ an - y wife?

Little Jumping Joan _____

Purpose   Control of fingers and thumbs, independently.

Position   Sitting with hands flat on floor, fingers straight, thumb tips touching.

Action   With thumb tips always touching, fingers gently fold under on first beats, out on third beats. Two actions to a measure.

25. LITTLE JUMPING JOAN

Polish melody (arr.)

Here am I: _____ lit - tle jump - ing Joan. When
no - bod - y's with me I'm al - ways a - lone.

Drums

Purpose Individualization of thumb and fifth. Arm turn.

Position Sitting on floor with backs of hands together, fingers spread, thumbs to floor for "Drums." For "Fife," palms together, fingers spread, fifths pointing toward the floor.

Action Hands turn in three beats. Thumb tips touch the floor in three beats on "Drums"; tips of fifth fingers touch the floor in three beats for "Fife." Four actions to each measure (three beats and one turn).

26. DRUMS

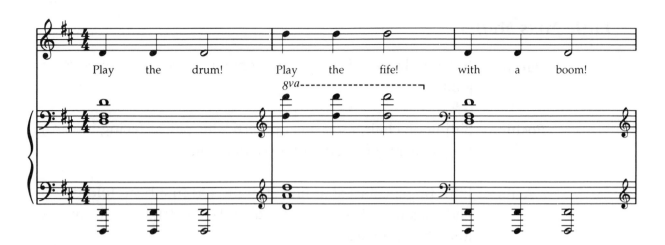

Little Miss Muffet

Purpose	Independence of finger movement. Flexibility of second joints.
Position	Sitting on chair, forearms up vertically, palms facing inward, fingers gently folded with tips touching.
Action	Fifth fingers start standing straight. On first beat, fold down and back from first and second joints. At "frightened," hands jump behind back.

27. LITTLE MISS MUFFET

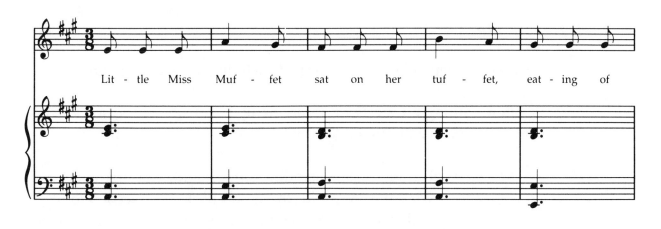

Lit - tle Miss Muf - fet sat on her tuf - fet, eat - ing of

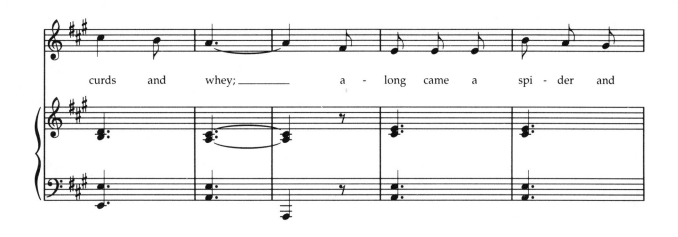

curds and whey; _____ a - long came a spi - der and

sat down be - side her and fright-ened Miss Muf - fet a - way!

Jack Be Nimble _____

Purpose   Independence, flexibility of each finger's second joint.

Position   Sitting on the floor, forearms up vertically, palms to center, apart, with fingers gently curved.

Action   Fourth fingers start standing up straight. On first beats of first two measures, fold down and back from second joints. On fourth beats of first two measures, fourths straighten. On the word "candle," hands drop to floor.

28. JACK BE NIMBLE

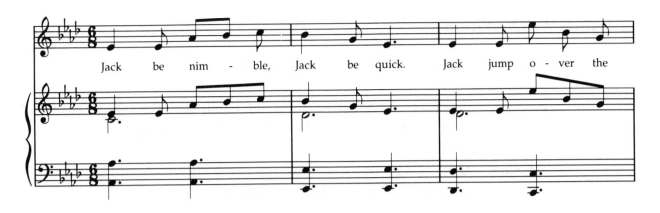

Jack be nim - ble, Jack be quick. Jack jump o - ver the

can - dle - stick!

Willy, Willy Wilkin _____

Purpose   Coordination. Wrist and hand freedom.

Position   Standing, the arms at shoulder level, straight out to sides, hands hanging loosely from wrists, fingers limp.

Action   Arms shake up and down, loosely, from shoulders. Four "down" movements to each measure.

29. WILLY, WILLY WILKIN

Wil - ly, Wil - ly Wil - kin kissed the maids a - milk - ing. Fa la la, fa la la,

fa la la, fa la la. And with his mer - ry daff - ing he set them all a - laugh - ing.

Ha ha ha, ha ha ha, ha ha ha, ha ha ha.

London Bridge Is Falling Down

Purpose   Wrist freedom. Action of forearms from elbow.

Position   Sitting on the floor, with arms stretched to front, hands flat on floor.

Action   On first beats of measure, begin a slow, fluid lifting of arms—forearms first, then raising hands, fingertips last to leave the floor. As arms drop back down, fingertips touch first, then wrists and arms.

Baby Shears

Purpose   Finger independence and control.

Position   Sitting on chair or floor, upper arms hanging from shoulder, with forearms straight out to front, hands extended with palms turned down. Acting fingers straight, others gently folded.

Action   On first beats of measures, fourth and fifth fingers straight, moving together, spread apart, then back together. Third and fourth fingers repeat the same motion.

30. LONDON BRIDGE IS FALLING DOWN

London Bridge is falling down, falling down, falling down;

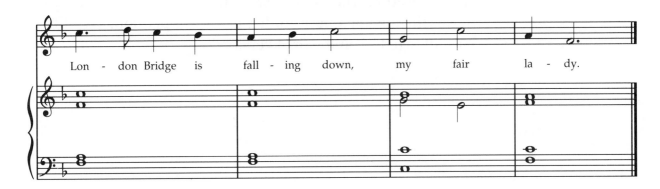

London Bridge is falling down, my fair lady.

31. BABY SHEARS

Shear the ___ sheep and trim the ___ tree, but let the lit - tle ___ lamb go free.

Farmer in the Dell _____

Purpose Control and coordination.

Position Sitting on the floor or chair, with forearms straight out to front, hands extended, palms down, fingers closed gently.

Action Actions begin on the first beat of measures. On the word "Farmer," fingers move out to straight position, then back to closed position. The thumbs start the action alone, then each of the fingers joins in, in order, at each repetition. Five fingers all together on the final version.

32. FARMER IN THE DELL

The farm - er in the dell, _____ the farm - er in the dell, _____
The farm - er takes a wife, _____ the farm - er takes a wife, _____
The wife _____ takes a child, _____ the wife _____ takes a child, _____
The child _____ takes a nurse, _____ the child _____ takes a nurse, _____
The nurse _____ takes a dog, _____ the nurse _____ takes a dog, _____

heigh - o the der - ry - o, the farm - er in the dell. _____
heigh - o the der - ry - o, the farm - er takes a wife. _____
heigh - o the der - ry - o, the wife _____ takes a child. _____
heigh - o the der - ry - o, the child _____ takes a nurse. _____
heigh - o the der - ry - o, the nurse _____ takes a dog. _____

Ride a Cock Horse

Purpose   Control. Hand freedom of movement.

Position   Standing, with arms at shoulder level, straight out to sides, hands hanging with fingers limp.

Action   On first beat of each measure, hands raise and drop in quick action from wrists, fingers limp.

33. RIDE A COCK HORSE

Ride a cock horse to Ban - bur - y Cross to see a fine la - dy up - on a white horse. Rings on her fin - gers, and bells on her toes, She shall have mu - sic wher - ev - er she goes.

Mulberry Bush

    Purpose   Thumb development and elasticity.

    Position   Sitting with upper arms hanging at side, forearms out straight to front, hands extended, palms up. Fingers together straight, thumbs across palms.

    Action   On first beats, thumbs begin to raise and rotate across palms in large, circular movement. One circular movement to each measure.

34. MULBERRY BUSH

Tick Tock _____

Purpose   Coordination. Balance. Freedom of movement.

Position   Sitting on the floor, hands in playing position rest gently on floor.

Action   On first beats, hands rock back and forth from side to side— from thumb to fifth finger. Fifth is touching on first measure, thumb on second.

35. TICK TOCK

Tick tock, tick tock, see the clock and hear its song; tick tock, tick tock, it will sing the whole day long; tick tock, tick tock.

Learning by Ear

Position   Playing position at the piano—preferably standing.
Presentation by rote.

Hands   Note-stems *up* indicate *right* hand.
Note-stems *down* indicate *left* hand.

Fingering
- Single notes: third fingers.
- Consecutive single notes: consecutive single fingers.
- Sustained three notes, played together, "Pussy Cat"—three fingers, left hand. (Soft stroking motion, suggestive of stroking the kitty.)
- Staccato two notes, played together, "Bouncer"—two fingers, right hand. (Free-arm staccato.)

Group I

1. Baby Bunnies
2. Jenny Wren
3. Mister G
4. Hear the Bell
5. Bob-White
6. Mister D
7. Turkey
8. Barn Owl
9. Tumbling Clowns

Group II

1. G's Voices
2. Woodpecker
3. Good Morning
4. Walking
5. Great Grey Owl
6. Lazy Frog

Group III

1. Swinging
2. Giant Steps
3. Bob-o-link
4. Short-Earred Owl
5. Good Afternoon
6. Hop-Toad

Group IV

1. This Is B
2. Three Little Kittens
3. Good Night
4. Pony Trots
5. Cuckoo
6. Big Balloons

Group V

1. Big Clock
2. Teeter-Totter
3. May Day
4. Dancing
5. Humming Birds
6. Pussy Cat

Group VI

1. Children
2. Whip-poor-will
3. Up the Street
4. Thrush
5. Skylark
6. Bouncer

Group VII

1. Mister Wren
2. Ding Dong Bell
3. Robin
4. Drums
5. An Old Dance

GROUP I

1. BABY BUNNIES

Hop! Hop! Hop! | Hop! Hop! Hop! | Ba - by Bun-nies. | Hop! Hop! Hop!

2. JENNY WREN

Jen - ny Wren, | Jen - ny Wren, | Dear sweet Jen - ny | sing a - gain.
(or: Jen - ny Wren)

3. MISTER G

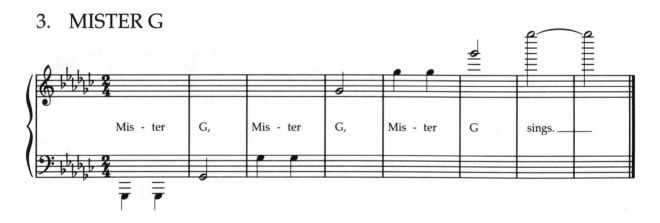

Mis - ter G, | Mis - ter G, | Mis - ter G | sings. ___

4. HEAR THE BELL

Hear the Bell, Hear it ring; tell - ing us 'tis time to sing.

5. BOB-WHITE

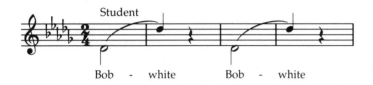

Student

Bob - white Bob - white

Teacher

Hear him call - ing, Thru the me - a - dow Bob - white, Bob - white

Student

Teacher

call - ing to his mate.____ Bob - white Bob - white

Student

6. MISTER D

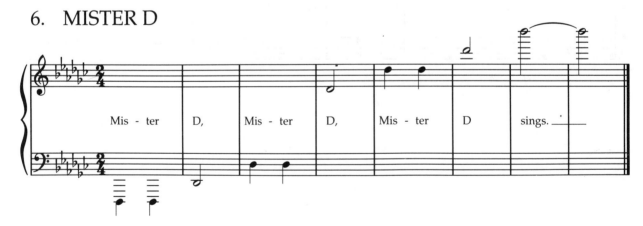

Mis - ter D, Mis - ter D, Mis - ter D sings.____

7. TURKEY

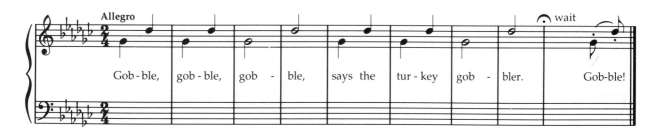

Gob-ble, gob-ble, gob-ble, says the tur-key gob - bler. Gob-ble!

8. BARN OWL

9. TUMBLING CLOWNS

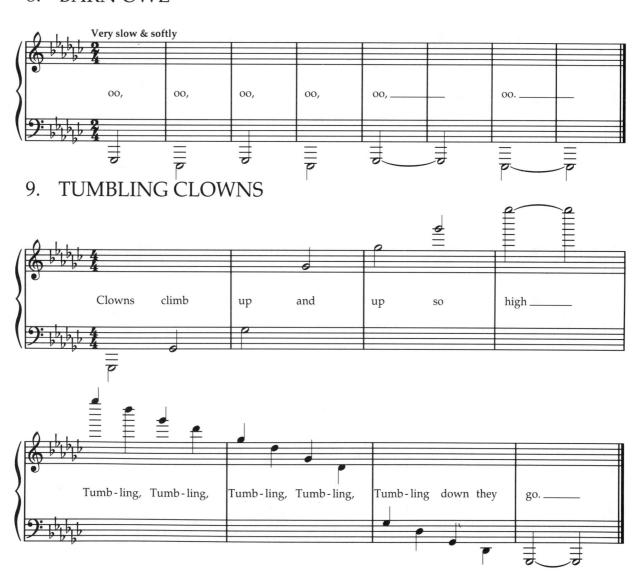

oo, oo, oo, oo, oo, ____ oo. ____

Clowns climb up and up so high ____

Tumb - ling, Tumb - ling, Tumb - ling, Tumb - ling, Tumb - ling down they go. ____

177

GROUP II

1. G'S VOICES

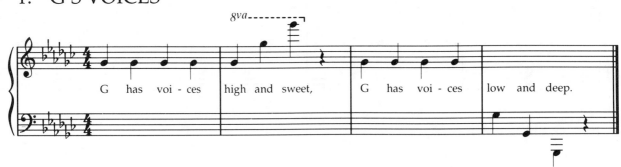

G has voi - ces high and sweet, G has voi - ces low and deep.

2. WOODPECKER

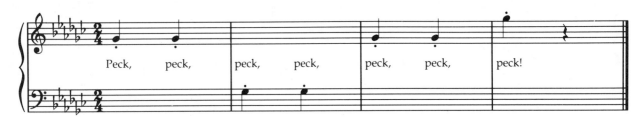

Peck, peck, peck, peck, peck, peck, peck!

3. GOOD MORNING

Good morn-ing, good morn-ing, good morn-ing to you!

4. WALKING

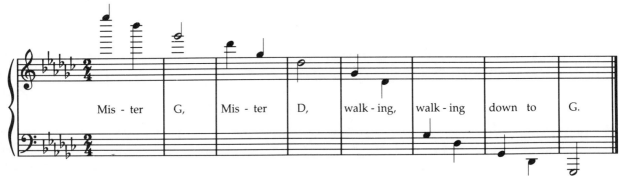

Mis - ter G, Mis - ter D, walk - ing, walk - ing down to G.

5. GREAT GREY OWL

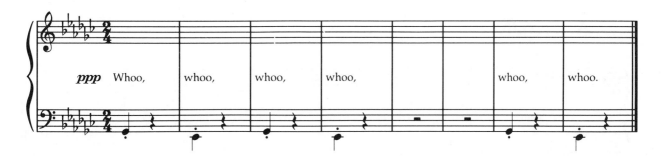

6. LAZY FROG

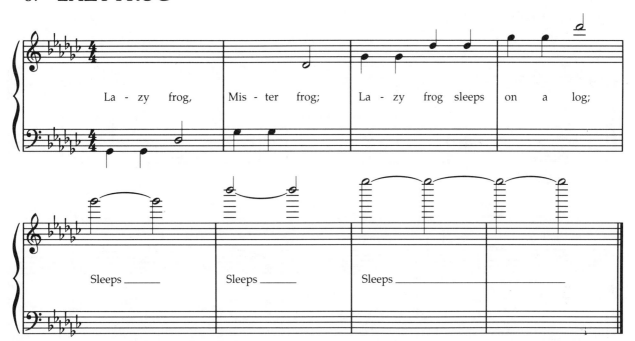

GROUP III

1. SWINGING

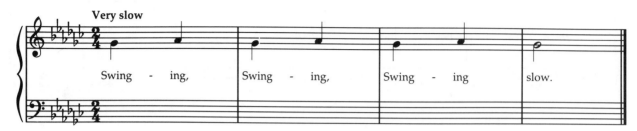

Swing - ing, Swing - ing, Swing - ing slow.

2. GIANT STEPS

Gi - ant steps are Great big steps, be - cause They're Great big gi - ants!

3. BOB-O-LINK

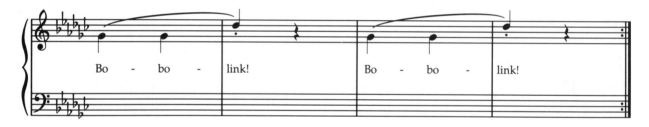

Bo - bo - link! Bo - bo - link!

4. SHORT-EARRED OWL

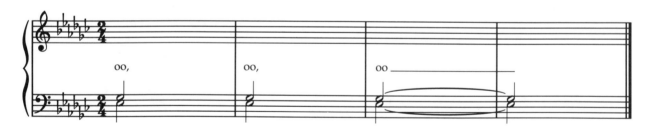

oo, oo, oo

5. GOOD AFTERNOON

Good Af-ter-noon, Good Af-ter-noon, Good Af-ter-noon to you.

6. HOP-TOAD

pp Hop - toad hid - ing in the grass, goes

Hop! Hop! Hop!

GROUP IV

1. THIS IS B

This is B, One, two, three, This is B's Song.

2. THREE LITTLE KITTENS

Meow, meow, meow, meow, meow, meow.

3. GOOD NIGHT

pp Good night, good night, good night, good night.

4. PONY TROTS

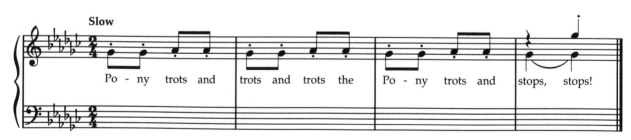

Po - ny trots and trots and trots the Po - ny trots and stops, stops!

5. CUCKOO

Cuc - koo, Cuc - koo, Cuc - koo, Cuc - koo.

6. BIG BALLOONS

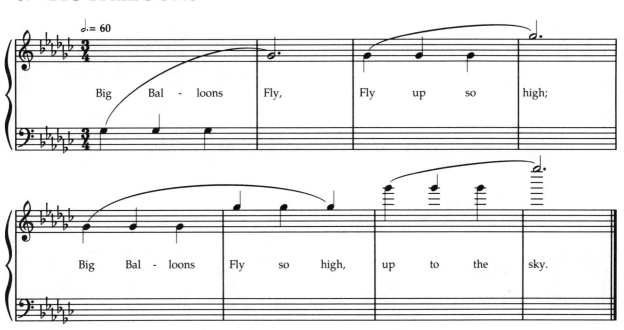

Big Bal - loons Fly, Fly up so high;

Big Bal - loons Fly so high, up to the sky.

GROUP V

1. BIG CLOCK

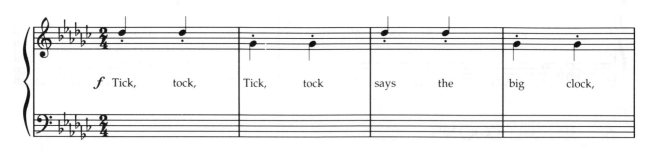

f Tick,   tock,   Tick,   tock   says   the   big   clock,

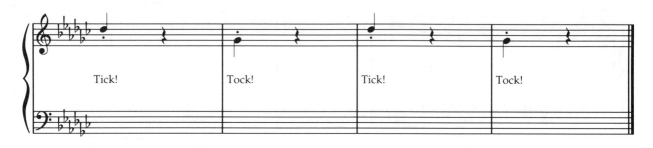

Tick!   Tock!   Tick!   Tock!

2. TEETER-TOTTER

Slow

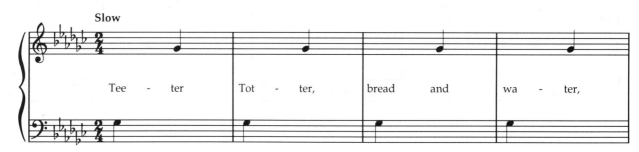

Tee - ter   Tot - ter,   bread   and   wa - ter,

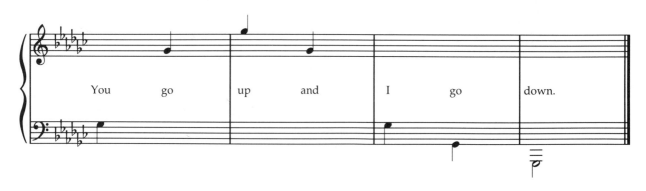

You   go   up   and   I   go   down.

3. MAY DAY

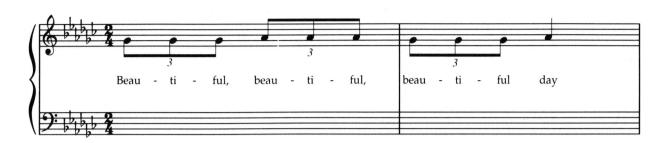

Beau - ti - ful, beau - ti - ful, beau - ti - ful day

Beau - ti - ful, beau - ti - ful, May - Day

4. DANCING

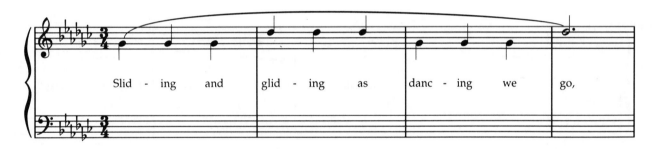

Slid - ing and glid - ing as danc - ing we go,

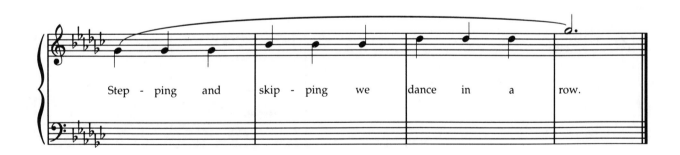

Step - ping and skip - ping we dance in a row.

5. HUMMING BIRDS

Hum - ming birds, hum - ming birds, hum - ming birds, Hum,

Hum, Hum, Hum, Hum.

6. PUSSY CAT

Pus - sy cat sits in the cor - ner all day; Pus - sy cat sings in this strange sort of way;

Purr Purr Purr

decrescendo

GROUP VI

1. CHILDREN

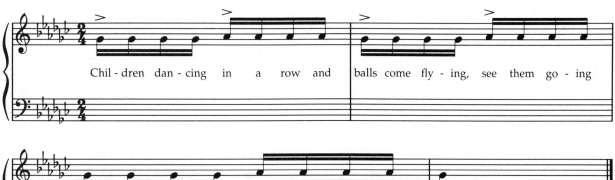

Chil - dren dan - cing in a row and balls come fly - ing, see them go - ing

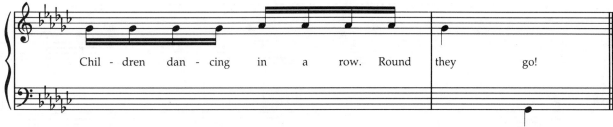

Chil - dren dan - cing in a row. Round they go!

2. WHIP-POOR-WILL

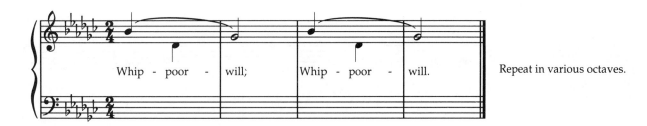

Whip - poor - will; Whip - poor - will.

Repeat in various octaves.

3. UP THE STREET

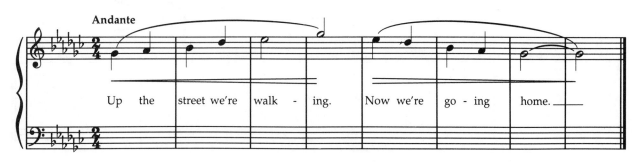

Andante

Up the street we're walk - ing. Now we're go - ing home.

4. THRUSH

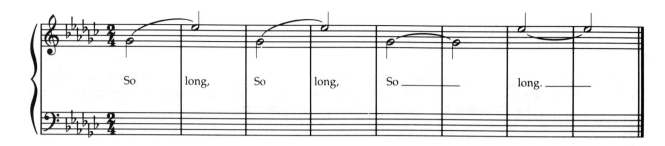

So long, So long, So ___ long. ___

5. SKYLARK

pp

6. BOUNCER

My dog-gie's name is Boun-cer; and Boun-cer says,

Bow - wow, Bow - wow, Bow - wow!

GROUP VII

1. MISTER WREN

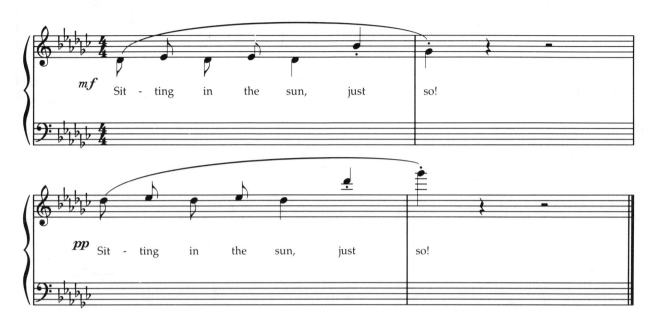

2. DING DONG BELL

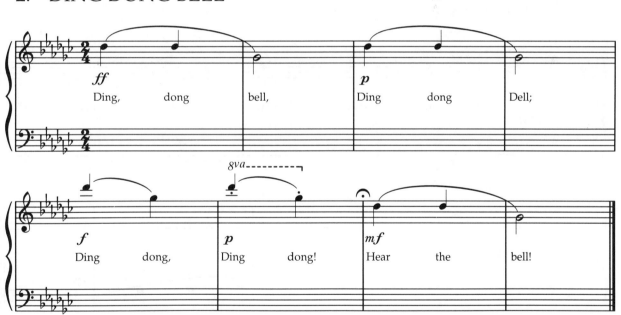

3. ROBIN

Lightly ♩. = 69

ppp Chee - ri - ly, Cheer up! Chee - ri - ly, Cheer up!

4. DRUMS

Play the drums, Play the drums, Play the drums for March - ing.

Play the drums, Play the drums, Play the drums and March. _

5. AN OLD DANCE

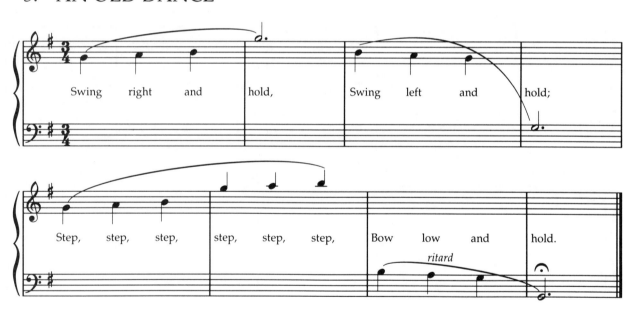

Swing right and hold, Swing left and hold;

Step, step, step, step, step, step, Bow low and hold.

ritard

Music   *Alfred's Basic Piano Library, Preparatory Course.* Willard Palmer, Morton Marus, and Amanda Vick Lethco. Van Nuys, CA: Alfred.

A Dozen a Day: Mini and Preparatory. Edna Mae Burnam. Florence, KY: Willis.

A First Piano Book for Little Jacks and Jills. Irene Rodgers. New York: G. Schirmer.

Introductory Pageants: Book I. Donald Waxman. Boston: Galaxy Music Corp., E. C. Schirmer.

Melody Maker I and II. Marcia Dunscomb, 300 Oak Street, Hollywood, FL 33019.

Music Lessons Have Begun. Leila Fletcher. Boston: Boston Music Co.

Musical Moments: Books I and II. Jon George. Miami: CPP/Belwin.

Performance Party, Books A, B, C, D. Jane, Lisa, and Lori Bastien. San Diego: N. Kjos.

Piano Party, Books A, B, C, D. Jane, Lisa, and Lori Bastien. San Diego: N. Kjos.

Play the Piano. Bernice Frost. Boston: Boston Music Co.

Primer Holiday Book. Cory. Dayton, OH: Lorenz Corp.

Primer Level Piano Student. Donald Glover and Louise Garrow. Miami: CPP/Belwin.

Songs and Silhouettes. MacCarteney. Florence, KY: Willis.

Duets

Easy for Me. Samuel Wilson. Boston: Boston Music Co.

Easy for Two. Louise Garrow. New York: G. Schirmer.

Two at One: Books I and II. Jon George. Miami: CPP/Belwin.

Workbooks   Music and Guide to *My Music Picture Book.* Sister Xavaria. Cincinnati: Willis.

Music for the Mini: Book II, Theory. Sue Ann Steck. Dayton, OH: Lorenz Corp.

My First Writing Book. Dorothy Crocker. Florence, KY: Willis.

My Music Color Book. Sister Xavaria. Florence, KY: Willis.

My Music Letter Book. Sister Xavaria. Florence, KY: Willis.

My Music Picture Book. Sister Xavaria. Florence, KY: Willis.

Theory and Ear Training Party, Books A, B, C, D. Jane, Lisa, and Lori Bastien. San Diego: N. Kjos.

Abramson, Robert M. *Rhythm Games for Perception and Cognition*. Vol. 1. Miami: CPP/Belwin, 1973.

American Dalcroze Journal. Dalcroze Society of America. Arizona State University, West Campus, 4701 West Thunderbird Road, P.O. Box 37100, Tempe, AZ.

Aronoff, Frances. *Music and Young Children*. New York: Turning Wheel Press (4 Washington Square Village, NYC 10012), 1982.

Ashton-Warner, Sylvia. *Teacher*. New York: Simon & Schuster, 1963.

Athey, Margaret, and Gwen Hotchkiss. *A Galaxy of Games for the Music Class*. New York: Parker, 1975.

Barnett, David. *The Performance of Music*. New York: Universe, 1972.

Berger, Kathleen Stassen. *The Developing Person*. 3d edition. New York: Worth, 1991.

Blockema, Mary. *The Marvelous Music Machine: A Story of the Piano (for the Young Child)*. Englewood Cliffs, NJ: Prentice-Hall, 1984.

Bruner, Jerome S. *The Process of Education*. New York: Random House/Vintage, 1960.

———. *Toward a Theory of Instruction*. Cambridge, MA: Harvard University Press/Belknap, 1966.

———. *The Relevance of Education*. New York: Norton, 1971.

———. *On Knowing: Essays for the Left Hand*. Expanded edition. Cambridge, MA: Harvard University Press/Belknap, 1979.

Casals, Pablo (as told to Albert E. Kahn). *Joys and Sorrows: Reflections*. New York: Simon & Schuster, 1970.

Choksey, Lois. *The Kodály Method*. Englewood Cliffs, NJ: Prentice-Hall, 1974.

Cuisenaire Materials for Learning Mathematics and Science (Cuisenaire Rods to help teachers help children learn music). Cuisenaire Co. Catalogue. New Rochelle, NY: Cuisenaire Co. of America, Inc. (12 Church Steet, Box D, New Rochelle, NY 10802).

Fine, Larry. *The Piano Book: A Guide to Buying a New or Used Piano*. Jamaica Plain, MA: Brookside, 1987.

Gardner, Howard. *Frames of Mind*. New York: Basic Books, 1985.

Highet, Gilbert. *The Art of Teaching*. New York: Vintage, 1959.

Jacques-Dalcroze, Emile. *Rhythm, Music, and Education*. Trans. Harold F. Rubenstein. London: The English Dalcroze Society, 1967.

Kaplan, Barbara, ed. *Kodály: A Dynamic Tradition (The Kodály Concept: A Bibliography for Music Education)*. Whitewater, WI: Organization of American Kodály Educators, 1985.

Landeck, Beatrice. *Songs to Grow On and More Songs to Grow On.* New York: Marks and Sloane, 1950.

Matthay, Tobias. *The Act of Touch in All Its Diversity.* London: Bosworth, 1903.

————. *The Visible and Invisible in Pianoforte Technique.* London: Oxford University Press, 1932.

Montessori, Maria. *Dr. Montessori's Own Handbook.* Rochester, VT: Schenkman, 1965.

Rivera, A. Ramon, and Thelma Gruenbaum. *To: Music and Children With Love.* Brookline, MA: exPress All, 1979.

Steinitz, Toni. *Teaching Music in Rhythmic Lessons: Theory and Practice of the Dalcroze Method.* Tel Aviv: "Or-Tav" Music Publications (available through Musik Innovations, 9600 Perry Highway, Pittsburgh, PA 15237).

Suzuki, Shinichi. *Nutured by Love.* New York: Exposition, 1969.

Uszler, Marienne, Stewart Gordon, and Elyse Mach. *The Well-Tempered Keyboard Teacher.* New York: Schirmer Books, 1991.

Wilson, Frank R., and Franz L. Roehmann, eds. *Music and Child Development.* St. Louis: MMB Music (10370 Page Industrial Boulevard, St. Louis, MO 63132), 1990.

Yurko, Michiko. *No-H-in-Snake.* Van Nuys, CA: Alfred, 1973.

Index

Italicized page numbers refer to musical compositions.